If Saddlebags Could Talk

If Saddlebags Could Talk

METHODIST STORIES AND ANECDOTES

Frederick E. Maser
Robert Drew Simpson

PROVIDENCE HOUSE PUBLISHERS
Franklin, Tennessee

Printed in the United States of America

02   01   00   3   4   5

Library of Congress Catalog Card Number: 98-67800

ISBN: 1-57736-121-0

Cover design by Gary Bozeman

"Where Cross the Crowded Ways of Life" from
the *Methodist Hymnal*, 1905.

PROVIDENCE HOUSE PUBLISHERS
238 Seaboard Lane • Franklin, Tennessee 37067
800-321-5692
www.providencehouse.com

We dedicate this book
of Methodist stories to our wives

Mary Louise Maser

and

Megan Demarest Simpson

who have shared our interest in Methodist history.
As always they remain our inspiration.

Contents

Foreword   ix
Acknowledgments   xi

Part One—Early Methodism
       Until the Death of Asbury in 1816   3
Introduction   5
1. The Wesleys and Their Followers   7
2. Bishop Francis Asbury   18
3. Bishops, Preachers, and Laity   27

Part Two—American Methodism:
       Growing as the Nation Grew, 1816–1920   45
Introduction   47
4. The Bishops   49
5. The Circuit Riders   56
6. Life in the Churches   71
7. Women in the Church   86

8. Camp Meetings   97
9. Missions   103

Bibliography   113
About the Authors   115

Foreword

Frederick E. Maser and Robert Drew Simpson are well acquainted with the history of The United Methodist Church and its predecessors. Both have been students of Methodism for many years and both have written extensively about its history, including the stories of the people and events which are central to its heritage. Therefore, it is fitting that they have combined their talents and knowledge to produce this delightful volume of historical vignettes.

Maser and Simpson remind us that history is not only informative and inspirational, but also entertaining. Those interested in Methodist history will be interested in this volume with its stories about some whose names are very familiar to us and others about whom we have never heard. All are part of the rich and colorful tapestry of our history. You will enjoy reading about them.

Charles Yrigoyen Jr., General Secretary
General Commission on Archives and History
The United Methodist Church

Acknowledgments

We are grateful to several who supported and encouraged us in our endeavor to share our collection of Methodist stories. Especially do we thank Charles Yrigoyen Jr., General Secretary of the General Commission on Archives and History; Dale Patterson, Archivist for the General Commission; and Mark Shenise, Associate Archivist. We are also grateful to Leonard Sweet, dean of the Drew Theological School; Kenneth Rowe, professor of church history and Methodist Librarian, Drew Theological School; and Ernest S. Lyght, Bishop, the New York area, United Methodist Church.

In addition, Megan Demarest Simpson has provided valuable counsel not only in the writing and the development of our work, but also in computer assistance. We deeply appreciate her contribution.

If Saddlebags Could Talk

Part One

Early Methodism
Until the Death of Asbury in 1816

Introduction

History is the oral or written record of persons and peoples. If this definition seems too narrow, it at least has the advantage of aim and brevity. When thinking of Methodist history, it is sufficiently broad to bring under its heading what the Methodists did, how they reacted to the social and religious mores of their day, and what kind of impact they made on the generations they influenced. It also is sufficiently broad to include what effect the social world in which Methodism operated had on the Methodist people, their beliefs and their manner of living.

Although some of the stories that follow are amusing, their sole purpose is not to entertain but rather to reveal the heart, spirit, and some of the beliefs of Methodism in its earliest years. There are no doctrinal discussions here, no descriptions of the chronology of Methodist history, and no comparison of Methodist teaching with that of other denominations. The stories rather reflect the life of Methodism. They also reveal little-known facts and truths about Methodist leaders as well as about those sitting in Methodist pews. The book is meant to give the reader a feel for Methodism based on Methodist lives rather than on Methodist doctrine or teaching. The stories, although arranged chronologically, are grouped in broad categories for easy reading.

Inspiration for our story approach to Methodism comes from the Roman Catholic theologian, G. K. Chesterton, who, as the creator of the Father Brown mysteries, knew a good story when he heard one. Chesterton wrote, "What holds families together is not so much the Ten Commandments or undying love as family jokes; these are the esoteric bonds, like secret passwords, known only to the family and showing life as it was really lived."

The material is presented in two sections. The first section—*Early Methodism: Until the Death of Asbury in 1816*—is comprised of stories about the Wesleys and some who were close to them, both great and small. There are a number of stories about Bishop Francis Asbury, which reveal his strengths and his weaknesses. The largest collection in this section focus on stories about early bishops, circuit riders, and the laypeople, who thrived or sometimes suffered, under them, and vice versa.

The second section is entitled—*American Methodism: Growing as the Nation Grew, 1816–1920*. In the main, the stories presented in both sections are from the regular columns we have written over the years for *Methodist History* and *Historians Digest* at the invitation of the United Methodist Commission on Archives and History. "If saddlebags could talk," this is what they would say.

Chapter 1

The Wesleys and Their Followers

WESLEY BAREFOOT—A LESSON FOR PROUD BOYS

When John Wesley was in Georgia, he and his friend Delamotte were teaching in separate schools. Some of Delamotte's boys wore shoes and stockings, and thought themselves superior to Wesley's boys who came to school barefoot. To cure their pride, Wesley changed schools with his friend. At the first class Wesley showed up barefoot. The boys were stunned when Wesley, without comment, walked about the class barefoot, and kept them at their lessons. But they got the message. Before the end of the week he cured their vanity.

SAMUEL WESLEY'S WIT

Samuel Wesley Sr. was distinguished for his ironic wit. He also was a master at improvisation. The two gifts came together at a banquet given for Wesley and a few friends by a miserly character who lived near Epworth. Everyone was astounded at the sudden generosity of the miser. He requested Samuel Wesley to return thanks after the meal. Wesley obliged with the following:

Behold a miracle! for 'tis no less
Then eating manna in the wilderness!
Here some have starved where we have found relief,
And seen the wonders of a chine of beef;
Here chimnies smoke which never smoked before,
And we have dined where we shall dine no more.

The miser confirmed the last line by saying, "No, gentlemen. It is too expensive."

The Difference

There were many ways in which John and Charles Wesley were different. In choosing preachers, Charles looked for gifts and talent while John emphasized grace. Charles wanted persons who could preach; John wanted persons who professed an experience in Christ and were willing to serve. Their differences are brought out in an amusing incident that took place in an early conference where a young preacher with great emotion was describing his religious experience.

"Stop that man from speaking," shouted Charles who seemed to feel that valuable time was being wasted. But the preacher continued as though he had not heard Charles's remark.

"Stop that man from speaking and let us attend to business," said Charles but the man continued to address the conference.

John, who was evidently enjoying the good brother's testimony, made no effort to stop him.

"Unless he stops," shouted Charles, "I'll leave the conference!"

"Reach him his hat!" said John, thus effectively cooling his brother's temper.

Charles did not leave, but he probably churned inwardly and sat back under protest. It was only one of many times that John and Charles disagreed.

Self-Denial

On one occasion a rich Methodist invited John Wesley and one of his preachers for dinner. When they sat down in the dining room, they were a bit overwhelmed by the abundance of good things to eat. They had been invited to a feast that could have been provided only by a person of wealth.

The preacher who was with Wesley said with more self-righteousness than tact or politeness, "O sir! What a sumptuous dinner! Things are very different than what they were formerly. There is now little self-denial among the Methodists."

Wesley looked at his preacher for a moment and then pointing to the abundance of food on the table said quietly, "My brother, there is a fine opportunity for self-denial now."

There is no record indicating whether the brother denied himself the tasty dishes or enjoyed a good dinner. It would have been difficult to do both.

Female Preachers

Methodists are sometimes startled to learn that John Wesley was not opposed to females preaching. He especially encouraged those who knew how to preach and who were obviously called by God for this work. Among the last letters of John Wesley is one to a Miss A. Cambridge, an Irish Methodist who was only twenty-nine years of age. She had established several Class Meetings in the town of Bandon. She herself usually led in prayer and exhorted. She also held meetings in various nearby places. Some of the Methodists, and particularly some of the preachers, believed her work was entirely irregular and should not be tolerated. Their objection was not to her gifts and talents but to her sex. She was a woman. Concerned about the situation, she wrote to Wesley for advice. His answer is enlightening, and in some ways is amusing. He suggests that she should refrain from preaching near any Methodist preacher since she might draw away his crowd. The letter follows:

London, January 31st, 1791

My dear Sister,

I received your letter an hour ago. I thank you for writing so largely and so freely; do so always to me as your friend, as one that loves you well. Mr. Barber has the glory of God at heart; and so have his fellow labourers. Give them all honour, and obey them in all things as far as conscience permits. But it will not permit you to be silent when God commands you to speak; yet, I would have you give as little offense as possible; and, therefore, I would advise you not to speak at any place where a preacher is speaking at the same time, lest you should draw away his hearers. Also, avoid the first appearance of pride or magnifying yourself. If you want books, or anything, let me know; I have your happiness much at heart. During the little time I have to stay on earth, pray for,

Your affectionate brother,
John Wesley

The Art of Preaching

John Wesley did not preach with the rhetorical style of George Whitefield. However, he was always forceful in his presentation. Although he preached in a conversational manner, he preached with great earnestness. No one could hear a sermon by Wesley without feeling the emotional intensity of his preaching. In fact Wesley would have had little respect for a man whose preaching lacked emotional power.

On one occasion he and Samuel Bradburn were walking through Billingsgate Market. Suddenly they were disturbed by two women who were quarreling furiously and using language more vehement and vigorous than pious.

"Pray, let us go; I cannot stand it," said Bradburn. He began to hurry along faster to get away from the two women who were speaking with inspired but not heavenly language.

"Stay, Sammy," said Wesley, "and learn how to preach."

JOHN WESLEY'S WIT AND HUMOR

Wesley could hardly be labeled the Groucho Marx of his time, but he really was quite a wit. Some of his remarks do prompt a smile. For example, all of Wesley's sermons weren't "keepers" and he knew it. When this happened, he didn't hesitate to lay some blame on the backs of his hearers. In fact, his words could be withering. Once after preaching at Redriff Chapel he remarked, "it was a cold, uncomfortable place, to a handful of people who appeared to be just as much affected as the benches they sat upon."

On another occasion in 1757 Wesley described some of his hearers at Durham saying, "Three or four gentlemen put me in mind of the honest man at London, who was so cheerful and unconcerned while Dr. Sherlock was preaching about the Day of Judgement. Someone, amazed by the fellow's unconcern, asked, "Do you not hear what the Doctor is saying about the coming Judgement?" The man answered, "But it doesn't matter to me, for, you see, I am not of his Parish."

WESLEY'S WORD FOR POTENTIAL COUCH POTATOES

Did you know that Wesley published a book in 1747 entitled Primitive Physick? It is a fascinating collection of remedies for everything from abortion to baldness. Some of his suggestions might help deter us from becoming couch potatoes.

The section Wesley calls "Plain Easy Rules," which he copied from Dr. Cheyne's medical work, is overflowing with sound advice. In fact, the observations about exercise and personal hygiene are a kind of seventeenth-century Surgeon General's report.

Here is a sampling of what Wesley called "Plain Easy Rules."

The great rule of eating and drinking is to suit the quality and quantity of the food to the strength of the digestion; to take always such a sort and such a measure as sits light and easy upon the stomach.

Water is the wholesomest of all drinks; it quickens the appetite and strengthens the digestion.

Strong, and most especially spirituous liquors, are a certain, though slow, poison.

A due degree of exercise is indispensably necessary to health and long life. Walking is the best exercise for those who are able to bear it; riding for those who are not.

We may strengthen any weak part of the body by constant exercise. Exercise, first, should always be on an empty stomach; secondly, should never be continued to weariness; thirdly, after it, we should take to cool by degrees, other-wise we shall catch cold.

The passions have a greater influence upon health than most people are aware of. All violent and sudden passions dispose to, or actually throw people into acute diseases. Till the passion which caused the disease is calmed, medicine is applied in vain.

The love of God, as it is the sovereign remedy of all miseries, so in particular it effectually prevents all the bodily disorders the passions introduce, by keeping the passions themselves within due bounds; and by the unspeakable joy and perfect serenity and tranquility it gives the mind, it becomes the most powerful of all the means of health and long life.

JOHN WESLEY AND TIME

John Wesley evidently lived by the New Testament counsel to "make the most of the time." Once he was kept waiting for his carriage. While he paced the roadside, someone near heard him mutter to himself, "I have lost ten minutes for ever."

On another occasion, when Wesley was dashing about, a friend commented, "You need not be in such a hurry." Wesley shot back, "A hurry, Sir, a hurry. Though I am always in haste, I am never in a hurry because I never undertake any more work than I can go through with perfect calmness of spirit."

The Wesleys and Their Followers

WHEN A FISHWIFE SAVED WESLEY'S NECK

On numerous occasions John Wesley needed a bodyguard to protect him from a mob. One of the more unlikely protectors emerged one day when he was preaching on the Exchange steps at New Castle. On this occasion the mob began pelting him with mud and rotten eggs. Suddenly a burly fishwife, the terror of the neighborhood, ran up the steps and threw her arm around Wesley's neck. Shaking her fist at the rioters, she shouted in a language they all understood, "If ony o'ye lift another hand to touch ma canny man ayle floor ye directly."

The crowd got her message and listened to Wesley's message.

WESLEY, WORSHIP, AND WOMEN

It is amazing how John Wesley seemed to have had rules for everything. The intent, of course, was to promote the spiritual welfare of the infant societies. Without discipline and direction Methodism may not have survived. To read some of these rules in contrast to what is practiced today among Methodists not only amuses, but also staggers the imagination. For instance, consider Wesley's directions for building and arranging the Methodist places of worship. Incorporated in these rules are those for sitting in church. Note especially those rules having to do with women.

1st. Build all preaching houses, where the ground will permit, in the octagon form. It is best for the voice, and on many accounts more commodious than any other.

2nd. Why should not an octagon house be built after the model of Yarm; any square house after the model of Bath or Scarborough? Can we find any better model?

3rd. Let the roof rise only one third of its breadth. This is the true proportion.

4th. Have doors and windows enough, and let all the windows be sashes opening downwards.

5th. Let there be no Chinese paling, and no tub pulpit, but a square projection, with a long seat behind.

6th. Let there be no pews, and no backs to the seats, which should have aisles on each side, and be parted in the middle by a rail running all along, to divide the men from the women.

Question 64. Is there any exception to the rule, "Let the men and women sit apart?"

Answer. In those galleries where they have always sat together, they may do so still; but let them sit apart every where below, and in all newly erected galleries.

But how can we secure this sitting apart? I must do it myself. If I come into any new house and see the men and women together I will immediately go out. I hereby give public notice of this. . . . pray let it be observed.

But there is a worse indecency than this creeping in among us— talking in the preaching houses before and after service.

Don't Burn Those Sermons—At Least Not the Good Ones

It is not just the mediocre or hassled preacher who grabs a sermon from the barrel to be warmed over and served to the waiting multitude. Some parishioners even call such sermons reruns. Indeed, John Wesley himself was not beneath recycling a good sermon. He spelled out his homiletical rationale for this practice in his journal for September 1, 1778.

Recalling a friend's remark that "he burned all his sermons every seven years; for it is a shame if he couldn't write better sermons now than he did seven years ago," Wesley observed, "Whatever others can do, I really cannot." As one example, Wesley said, "I can not write a better sermon on the Good Steward than I did seven years ago. I can not write a better sermon on the Use of Mercy than I did thirty years ago."

We may wager, however, that Wesley would agree that some sermons would provide more light and warmth if they were burned rather than preached.

What Is a "Good Methodist"?

Have you ever heard someone say, "I have always been a good Methodist." In some moment of exuberance we may even have said it ourselves. But do you ever wonder what a good Methodist is after all? What defines a Methodist?

Apparently John Wesley wrestled with that question and came up with an answer worthy of our attention. He wrote:

> The distinguishing marks of a Methodist are not his opinions of any sort. His assenting to this or that scheme of religion, his embracing any particular set of notions, his espousing the judgment of one man or of another are all quite wide of the point. Whosoever, therefore, imagines that a Methodist is a man of such and such an opinion, is grossly ignorant of the whole affair; he mistakes the truth totally.

> What then is the mark? Who is a Methodist according to your own account? I answer: A Methodist is one who has the love of God shed abroad in his heart: that he who loveth God loves his brother also. Loves not only God but loves his neighbor as himself, and does good unto all men, neighbors and strangers, friends and enemies.

> These are the principles and practices of our sect; these are the marks of a true Methodist. If any man say, "Why, these are only the common fundamental principles of Christianity!" Thou hast said; so I mean. This is the very truth. I know no other.

Thumbs-Up and Protestant Relics

George Whitefield (1714–1770), a member of Wesley's Holy Club at Oxford, followed the Wesleys as a missionary in Savannah, Georgia. However, a major difference between Whitefield and the Wesleys in America was that Whitefield was an immense success. As a father of the Great Awakening, he evangelized the colonists on the Eastern seaboard and became something of a Protestant saint.

When Whitefield died in 1770 in Newburyport, Massachusetts, he was buried in a crypt beneath the church. Because he was so venerated, people sought every opportunity to visit his tomb and to handle his bones. A number of prominent persons entered the tomb such as Benedict Arnold and some of his officers. The most ghoulish of visits is that one described by Menton Thrift in 1823 when Jesse Lee visited with some of his friends. Thrift described the occasion,

> They descended into the vault and upon opening the coffin, they were able to witness the fearful change which the king of terror makes upon the most perfect forms. They discovered his ears, hair, and a part of his nose had fallen off. His teeth were white, and fast in their sockets. His breast bone had parted, and his bowels disrobed. His wig and clothes were all decayed, except in a few places. Parts of his gown still remained. His flesh was black and destitute of comeliness. After visiting this dreary mansion, which contains the mortal part of one of the greatest missionaries that ever lived, Mr. Lee contented himself by bringing away a small relic of the gown in which he was buried, and prayed that he might be endued with the same zeal which once inspired the breast of its wearer.

But the tale is not finished. Years later the British reclaimed Whitefield's remains and were returned except his arm. Supposedly his arm remains entombed in Newburyport. The Methodist Museum at Drew University, however, claims to possess Whitefield's thumb! One wag insists that Whitefield's thumb is always up.

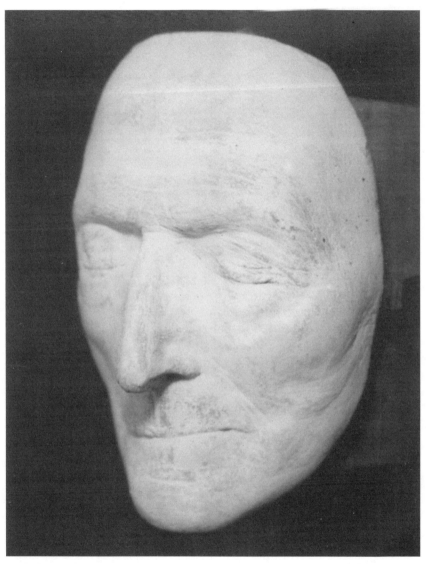

John Wesley's death mask.

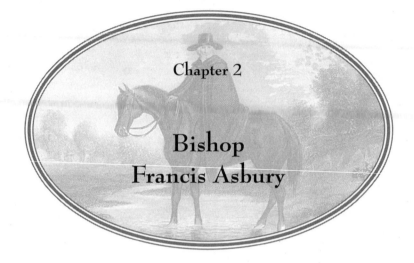

Chapter 2

Bishop
Francis Asbury

THE SECRET OF GREATNESS

Francis Asbury (1745–1816) was only about five-feet-nine-inches tall, but morally and spiritually he was a giant. He was by no means a great preacher, but his impact on the congregations to which he preached and on the men who served under him was without equal.

His weakness as a preacher can be illustrated by the amusing story of a time when he and Jesse Lee were traveling together. The Bishop had an appointment to preach about forty miles outside of Philadelphia. When the two men arrived, Bishop Asbury was not feeling well and he asked Lee to substitute for him. Lee was a powerful preacher and after his address the Bishop gave a brief exhortation. Some of the people said they liked the Bishop's sermon, but they did not care for what the old man said after him. They had mistaken Lee for the Bishop.

The Bishop's strength lay not in his preaching but in his sincerity and in his deep prayer life. At one time he set aside three hours out of each day for prayer. It is said that when men mocked him, his revenge was a prayer that God would bless them. He truly walked with God, and his favorite hymn was one by Cowper ending with the verse:

So shall my walk be close with God
Calm and serene my frame;
So purer light shall mark the road
That leads me to the Lamb.

ASBURY PAYS A DEBT

A sbury seldom received visitors or visited with friends without offering a prayer at the time of their departure. There is a mildly amusing incident of a time when Asbury was ill, and was attended by the famous Philadelphia physician, Dr. Benjamin Rush, and a colleague. When they completed their services, Asbury asked them for their bill. They respectfully replied that they wished no other recompense from Asbury than his prayers. They bowed and were about to depart when Asbury said that he always paid his debts promptly and that he would discharge his debt without delay. He immediately knelt down and fervently prayed for the conversion of his two medical friends.

The two physicians were taken by surprise. Dr. Rush, who was an intimate friend of Asbury and widely noted not only for his skill as a physician but also for his Christian piety, was more than delighted with Asbury's prayer, especially since it brought Dr. Rush's skeptical colleague to his knees. The skeptic was exceedingly embarrassed to listen to a prayer offered to a Savior in whom he had no faith. The historian who records the incident does not relate what might have been the long term impact on the skeptics but he does point out that Asbury was prompt in paying his debts.

ASBURY THE DICTATOR

It is said that Asbury was a born autocrat. Coming to America in a day when people were shouting watchwords of democracy, he hadn't any idea of the meaning of the word. He expected immediate and complete obedience. Even when he urged his preachers to share their ideas with him, he never so much as gave their suggestions a thought, other than possibly to do something opposite to what they advised.

Once Bishop Asbury said publicly, "Brethren if any of you should have anything peculiar in your circumstances that should be known to the superintendent in making your appointment, if you will drop me a note, I will, as far as will be compatible with the great interests of the church, endeavor to accommodate you."

One man wrote him requesting that he be appointed in the west where he had relatives who would make his work more pleasant. Not only the man's request was not answered, but he was sent a hundred miles east. He said to the bishop later, "If that's the way you answer prayers you will get no more prayers from me." Asbury only shrugged his shoulders and said, "Well, be a good boy, James, and all things will work together for good."

For those who bowed to Asbury's will and gave him complete obedience life was a happy experience. But to the persons who failed to treat his word as law, Asbury could be as cold as ice and hard as stone.

He was an anomaly—a dictator in a democracy.

ASBURY AND THE PLEA FOR POVERTY

The early Methodist preachers received an allowance not a salary. In fact, they prided themselves on not acquiring wealth through their calling. Asbury himself greatly feared the effects that wealth might have on piety. However, he was solicitous of his preachers, and when he found any in dire poverty he shared his own income with them. On one occasion he gave a valuable watch to a preacher who was destitute.

On the other hand, Asbury was at times overzealous in his emphasis on the evils of riches. He probably had forgotten that it is the love of wealth and not wealth itself that is to be feared. One time he prayed publicly to God to keep the preachers poor. A critic said that it was an unfortunate prayer to have uttered in that particular place since the inhabitants of that area did everything in their power to keep the preachers poor and needed no help from God for that purpose.

Some people believed that the preachers should remain poor so they could understand the trials of some of their parishioners. Certain mothers advised their daughters never to marry a Methodist preacher since the preacher and his wife would only have "books and babies."

At any rate, Asbury's prayer was answered as far as early Methodist preachers were concerned. They remained poor with a few exceptions, and Asbury's prayer followed the Methodist movement well into the nineteenth century.

BISHOP ASBURY, MARRIAGE, AND THE CHILDREN

The question of why Francis Asbury never married has often been raised. But his reasoning is clear. He felt it unfair to bind a woman to a husband who was destined to be away fifty-one weeks of the year. As he said, "It is neither just nor generous."

This does not mean, however, that Asbury scorned family, or children in particular. There are ample letters to prove, for instance, that he viewed Mary Garrettson, the daughter of Catherine and Freeborn, almost as a daughter. His will notes that many children were named for him, and this gave him a deep sense of pride.

Children in general seemed to warm to his playfulness and affection. There is a priceless note from one child's remembrance. This youngster ran home and breathlessly shouted, "Mother, I want my face washed and a clean apron on, for Bishop Asbury is coming and I am sure he will hug me up."

QUESTIONABLE RECRUITS

Peter Cartwright (1785–1872) was a rugged, homespun preacher who had little use for educated preachers. It is no wonder that he recalled especially a great revival in one of the western conferences where a number of wealthy and well-educated people were converted. Two of them felt the call to preach. They were enthusiastically received by the conference. Bishop Asbury, however, sat

Francis Asbury's consecration as bishop, Christmas Conference, Lovely Lane Chapel, Baltimore, Maryland, 1784.

throughout the session with his eyes almost closed. Cartwright described the outcome with great satisfaction.

> After they were received he (Asbury) seemed to wake up. "Yes, yes!" he exclaimed, "in all probability they both will disgrace you and themselves before the year is out." And sure enough, in six months one was riding the circuit with a loaded pistol and a dirk, threatening to shoot and stab the rowdies; the other was guilty of a misdemeanor, and in less than nine months they were both out of the church.

Asbury, according to Cartwright, often said to his preachers, "You read books, but I read men."

Colonel Asbury

The circuit rider's life on the frontier was in constant peril. Disease and accidents were commonplace and on occasion he fell into the midst of settler and Indian warfare. In 1793 Bishop Asbury faced such an experience in western Pennsylvania. There was a series of Indian raids on the frontier. Therefore it was the practice of the preachers to band together as they traveled. In this instance Asbury and a party of armed preachers were traveling through 130 miles of wilderness. Hostile Indians were in pursuit.

What to do at nightfall in the event of attack?

Rev. William Burke, who was in the party, gave this account. "We were all pretty well armed except the Bishop." However, Asbury planned a strategy for defense when they camped at nightfall. Burke explains that they were to "make a rope long enough to tie to the trees all around the camp except a small passage for us to retreat. . . . the rope to be so fixed as to strike the Indians below the knee, in which case they would fall forward, and we would retreat into the dark and pour our fire upon them from our rifles."

Fortunately the Indians never attacked. If they had attacked, Asbury and his preachers may have become only a footnote in Methodist history.

Asbury had many sterling qualities, but he was no Napoleonic General, not even a Colonel.

Bishop Francis Asbury and the Wisdom of Stepping Down

Bishop Asbury is sometimes characterized as an autocratic leader, and there is much evidence to substantiate this observation. However, his exercise of strict authority did not prevent him from recognizing that a time comes to relinquish authority. His wisdom in knowing when and how to step down from leadership might well be emulated. Asbury's thoughts are documented in two unpublished letters written to the Rev. Freeborn Garrettson (1752–1827) in 1811.

Asbury stated, "I feel it is not with me as in years past: the 50th year of my social exercises, 46th year of my traveling, 40th year in

America, 66th year of my life; I have with great pleasure stepped out of the presidential chair, not to return." Later, in January 1811, he further commented. "We must exercise patience, when our younger Brethren want to push away our feet. I feel unspeakable pleasure to take away my feet from the Chair of the Presidency in all our Conferences. I rejoice to see it better filled, and with more honor. We must learn to rise, shine, decline, and set with Dignity. It has been the weakness of some good men in church and state, not always to know when to step down a Little, and stop."

Bishop Asbury's Last Will and Testament

Asbury drafted his will June 7, 1813, three years before his death. This was understandable for his health was already precarious. Ill with rheumatism and tuberculosis, he was often on crutches and needed to be carried from his carriage by his traveling companion.

But what did this man have to leave? What was his legacy?

The will is comprised of four "Items." The first "Item" is a statement of the faith by which he lived. He states, "I give my body to the dust, from whence it was originally taken, in hopes of a Glorious resurrection to everlasting life! I commit my Spirit to the Father of all Spirits, in the justifying, sanctifying, preserving, and Glorifying Grace of the Son of God and only Saviour of the world."

Having affirmed his faith, Asbury attends to the practical considerations and needs of living. In "Item Two" he declares, "I give and bequeath all my wearing apparel to the traveling and local preachers of the Methodist E. Church that shall be present at my death." Imagine the thrill some young preacher must have felt when he preached, wearing the bishop's clothes.

Asbury knew how important transportation and learning were, especially to a bishop. Therefore, we are not surprised that "Item Three" states, "I give and bequeath my Horses or Horse and carriages, together with all my Books and Manuscripts, to William McKendree, first American Bishop of the Methodist E. Church." How practical that Asbury would leave his horses and his library to McKendree.

"Item Four" is divided in three parts. In the first part, Asbury leaves two thousand dollars "now deposited in the Book Concern to be applied in printing Bibles and Testaments, with other pious Books and Tracts and Pamphlets upon experimental and practical Godliness." Further, he directs that if "the present order of things be changed I wish the money to be funded, and the Interest by the Special Trust be equally and annually divided among the Ten Conferences, or if the number shall be increased, there shall be an equal dividend to the whole number."

The second part reveals that various persons had left legacies to Asbury to provide for him in his old age when he would need "an Independent support." If these monies are not needed, he wills as a "faithful steward" that the "Interest and some of the principal" be returned to the Church. Further, he makes an interesting and compassionate bequest to Elizabeth Dickins of eighty dollars annually should she "survive me and continue in her widowhood." She was the widow of Rev. John Dickins, Asbury's close friend and founder of the Book Concern, who had died in 1798 of yellow fever. Elizabeth Yancey Dickins had the honor of being the first woman to occupy a Methodist parsonage. Some wag might say that this may have been the reason for Asbury's act of compassion.

The final part of "Item Four" reveals his special concern for children. Asbury was very fond of children, and they were fond of him. Many were named for him. It is not surprising, therefore, that his Will directs, "As to all my nominal Children, Male and Female, whose parents have thought proper to put any part of my name upon them, I wish the Book Concern to give to each of these (children) each a Bible, as one of my nominal Children."

And what wishes did he express for his burial? Very simply he wrote, "my Burial decent and solitary, a Gravestone or not, but plain; my Funeral expenses paid by money in my Pocket, or from the Interest of the deposit in the Concern. Francis Asbury."

Who Says It and How

A half dozen persons may say the same thing and yet possibly only one may make a striking impact upon his or her audience. This truth is attested to by an incident in the life of Francis Asbury. On one occasion in the city of Albany, after having completed the ordination service, Asbury raised a Bible in his hand and said with a stirring emphasis, "This is the minister's battle-axe. This is his sword. Take this therefore and conquer."

Nathan Bangs, the Methodist historian who records the incident adds, "These same words might have been uttered by another and yet produced no effect. For it was not the words simply, but the manner and the occasion of using them which invested that . . . power which produced a thrilling effect."

On another occasion, being annoyed by the bright attire of one candidate for ordination and the self-confidence of another, Asbury suddenly burst out into a stream of rebuke combined with tender expostulations. The manner in which he spoke, says Bangs who also records this incident, "caused the ears of all who heard him to tingle, creating . . . a sudden sensation of abhorrence against everything beneath the dignity, the gravity, and the holiness of the ministerial character."

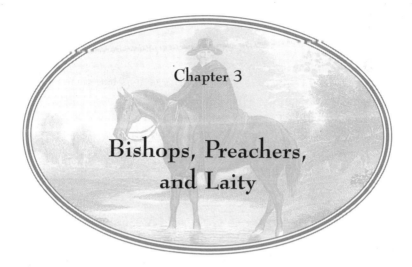

Chapter 3

Bishops, Preachers, and Laity

HOW WE GOT OUR NAME

Thomas Ware, a New Jersey Methodist preacher, was present at the Christmas Conference in 1784 when the Methodist Episcopal Church was founded. But how did they arrive at the name Methodist Episcopal Church? We can imagine why, but how did it really happen?

Ware, in the published sketches of his own life and ministry helps us answer the question. He attributes the name to the persuasive leadership of the Rev. John Dickens. Dickens, born and educated in England, had quickly gained prominence among his peers. In 1789, he founded the Methodist Book Concern, predecessor of the United Methodist Publishing House in Nashville, Tennessee, and became its first editor.

Ware recalled the discussion at the Christmas Conference when the question of a name for the new church arose. He recalled:

> The question arose, "What name or title shall we take?" I thought to myself, I shall be satisfied that we be denominated, "The Methodist Church," and so whispered to a brother sitting near me. But one proposed, I think it was John Dickens, that we should adopt the title of Methodist Episcopal Church. Mr. Dickens was in

the estimation of his brethren, a man of sound sense and sterling piety; and there were few men on the conference floor heard with greater deference than he. Most of the preachers had been brought up in what was called, "The Church of England," and, all agreeing that the plan of general superintendence, which had been adopted, was a species of episcopacy, the motion on Mr. Dickens'[s] suggestion was carried without, I think, a dissenting voice. There was not, to my recollection, the least agitation on the question.

The Preacher Got the Last Laugh

There are many stories about lawyers having a joke at the expense of Methodist preachers. Here is one case when the formidable Jesse Lee (1758–1816), the apostle of Methodism to New England, turned the table.

Somewhere between Boston, and Lynn, Massachusetts, Lee was overtaken by two lawyers as he was riding leisurely along. The lawyers set about to have some fun with the preacher. After a friendly greeting all three rode on together a lawyer on either side of Lee. The conversation went as follows:

1st Lawyer: "I believe you are a Preacher, sir?"
Lee: "Yes, I generally pass for one."
1st Lawyer: "You preach very often, I suppose?"
Lee: "Generally every day; frequently twice or more."
2nd Lawyer: "How do you find time to study, when you preach so often?"
Lee : "I study when riding, and read when resting."
1st Lawyer: "But do you not write your sermons?"
Lee : "No, not very often at least."
2nd Lawyer: "Do you not often make mistakes in preaching extemporaneously?"
Lee: "I do sometimes."
2nd Lawyer: "How do you do then? Do you correct them?"
Lee: "That depends upon the character of the mistake. I was preaching the other day, and I went to quote the text, 'All liars

28

shall have their part in the lake that burneth with fire and brimstone' and by mistake, I said 'All lawyers shall have their part—'"

2nd Lawyer: (interrupting him) "What did you do with that? Did you correct it?"

Lee: "O, no, indeed! It was so nearly true, I didn't think it worthwhile to correct it."

"Humph! said one of them (with a hasty and impatient glance at the other) "I don't know whether you are a knave or a fool!"

"Neither," he quietly replied, turning at the same time his mischievous eyes from one to the other; "I believe I am just between the two!"

STRONG FOR GOD OR STRONG IN GOD

There are numerous stories that illustrate the strength of the early circuit riders. In a sense, they had to be strong to survive the elements, not only the weather, but also persecution and illness. It became a familiar saying, for instance, for people to describe the weather by saying that it was so bad "no one was out save crows and Methodist preachers."

The circuit riders at times used their brawn "for God," never hesitating to use physical force if necessary. Peace at any price was not their motto. There is the story of a blacksmith who boasted that he was going to lick every preacher who came his way. When a Methodist circuit rider approached this smithy one day and dismounted his horse, the blacksmith dropped his tongs and shouted, "You've come for your licking I see."

Walking calmly up to the blacksmith, the Methodist preacher felled him with one blow. Then the preacher sat on the man's abdomen and began to beat a tune on his head with a riding stock. When the smithy begged to be released, the preacher refused to let him go until he had recited several hymns, after the preacher had said the Lord's Prayer, and the smithy had promised to come to meeting that very evening. Afterward the preacher said, "Believe me I truly beat the fear of God into his head."

On the other hand, there were people like the preacher Philip Gatch, who were not strong enough to take this kind of action. On one occasion, Gatch was waylaid on the way to his meeting and tarred and feathered. Some of the tar got in one of his eyes, destroying his sight. Nevertheless, he continued to his appointment. Here his friends aided him, and then Gatch knelt leading them in prayer for the souls of those who had abused him. His prayers, it is said, led to the conversion of at least two of his assailants.

These two stories offer examples of the two kinds of strength that these early circuit riders brought to their work of preaching and conversion—physical force and endurance in suffering. The first circuit rider was strong *for* the Lord while Philip Gatch was strong *in* the Lord!

HOW TO CATCH A THIEF

Lorenzo Dow was probably one of the most eccentric of the early Methodist circuit riders. For instance, he proposed marriage to a person named Peggy and then went off on a preaching tour, leaving his fiancée wondering whether he would ever come to claim her. But Dow eventually returned and they were married, living, we assume, happily together for many years.

On one occasion when Dow was staying at an inn, a man reported that his purse had been stolen from his room while he had been eating his dinner. Since no new guests had arrived and none had left in the interval, it was obvious that the thief was still among the guests and hangers-on at the inn. But how to catch him? The innkeeper consulted with Dow, who stated he could easily identify the thief.

Dow brought in a rooster and placing it in the center of the main room, covered it with a huge kettle that had been hanging on the hearth. Then he addressed the whole group that had been gathered by the innkeeper. He stated that he would put the room in complete darkness, shutting off every bit of light. In the darkness every person present was to step forward and rub his hand on the bottom of the kettle, and "when the thief touches the kettle," said Dow in his stern, sober voice, "the rooster will crow! And we will know who is the thief."

It was a solemn gathering that surrounded the turned-down kettle and the rooster beneath. Dow formed the group into a single line and then carefully extinguished all lights. One by one the group placed their hands upon the kettle. Nothing happened! There was no cry from the rooster! Dow called for lights, and then said, "Let each person put out their hand."

Everyone did. All but one person had a black smudge on their hands from the bottom of the kettle which was naturally covered with soot. Only one had a pure white hand. He had not touched the kettle, fearful the rooster would crow.

Dow looked triumphantly at the innkeeper, "There," he said "is your thief."

SLEEPERS

Some preachers have become annoyed when one of their congregation falls asleep while they are preaching. A certain preacher, observing that everyone but one woman was dozing during his sermon, quietly picked up his hat and saddlebags and just as quietly left the meeting and mounted his horse. When the lone woman who had remained awake asked him if he were going to return at a future date, he is supposed to have replied, "No! God never called me to preach to a people I cannot keep awake."

Jesse Lee usually handled sleepers more astutely. Once while he was preaching he noted that most of his congregation were asleep. He became increasingly annoyed, especially as he noted that a group gathered in the yard outside the house were making a great deal of noise with their conversations.

He attempted to continue, but unable to cope with the situation longer, he suddenly cried, "I'll thank the people in the yard not to talk so loud; they'll wake up the people in the house!"

Modern preachers seem to handle the problem with more humor. One said, "I am not annoyed when someone in my congregation falls asleep. This is a day of great tension, and if I can give a man or a woman a sound half hour nap on a Sunday morning they owe me! They should grasp my hand on the way out of meeting and say, "Pastor you are wonderful. I never slept so well in all my life!" Continuing in this tongue-in-cheek fashion he added, "There are recent statistics about people who fall asleep in church. If you'd take all the people who fall asleep in church and laid them end to end, they'd be a lot more comfortable."

THE STRENGTH OF THE LORD

A story told about an early Methodist preacher named Joseph Collins illustrates what some preachers faced by way of travel, hunger, and persecution. Nonetheless some of them managed to rejoice in "the strength of the Lord." Collins was such a man. A powerful preacher, he was at the same time a strong combatant.

One day while riding to an appointment, Collins was overtaken by a youth who began to complain about preachers. Not knowing whom he was speaking to, he vigorously berated a preacher named Collins, and announced he was riding to a Collins's meeting where he was going to wallop the preacher and put him in his place. Collins said nothing, but as they drew closer to the meeting place he asked quietly whether Collins had ever harmed the young man. The youth replied that he had never even met Collins.

"Then" said Collins, "we may as well have a test of strength here before we get to the meeting place. I am Joseph Collins!"

On saying this, Collins stepped toward the young man who was too astounded even to speak. Taking him by the scruff of his neck and the seat of his pants, he hurled him over a nearby fence.

The young man picked himself up, looked in dismay at Collins and then said, "If you will kindly hand my horse over to me, I'll be on my way!"

Many of the early itinerants rejoiced in "the strength of the Lord!"

⟫•◆•⟪

CONNUBIAL BLISS

Lorenzo Dow, the eccentric preacher, thought all women were like his wife, Peggy. Unfortunately, he would discover to his dismay that he could not been more wrong. Peggy loved Dow with a passionate love that followed him anywhere he chose to go. She understood him probably more than anyone else. She accompanied him on all the journeys of his itinerant ministry, regardless of the cost to her health. She died young, but one of her legacies to Dow and the world was her journal which to this day is entertaining reading. After a reasonable time of mourning, Lorenzo Dow decided he wanted to be married again. What he really wanted was another Peggy.

His method for choosing a wife was unique. At the close of an evening meeting he arose and said, "I have decided to assume the married state again. I am looking for a wife, and I will marry the first woman who stands after I finish this announcement."

Two women leaped to their feet, almost simultaneously. Dow looked at each one critically and then he said, pointing to one of the women, "I think this woman stood first. I'll marry her."

And he did. But the marriage was not a success. His wife made demands that Peggy would never have considered. Instead of following Dow wherever he went she ordered him around for her own benefit.

One day a neighbor of the Dows, probably in disgust with his own marriage, put up a sign on his property which read, The Women Rule Here!

Dow scowled at the sign one day and then went home and put up a sign on his property. It read, Here Too! Dow had discovered that all women were not Peggy Dow.

THE SMALL BOY

The early American Methodists had among their preachers a number of eccentrics. Usually they were very sincere persons, but sometimes they expressed themselves in ways that were not generally acceptable or humorous. Often the eccentric preacher was himself unaware of the humor. A story about Billy Hibbard offers an appropriate illustration.

On one occasion the secretary of the Conference was calling the roll. He read out the name of William Hibbard. There was no answer. The secretary looked up in surprise, and then thinking he had not talked loudly enough said in a clear strong voice, "William Hibbard!" Still there was no answer. At this the secretary, noticing that Hibbard was in the front row of the Conference, looked directly at him and fairly shouted, "William Hibbard!" Still no answer.

William McKendree, the presiding bishop, looked up and said, "Mr. Hibbard, will you please answer to your name!"
Hibbard looked up and said "That's not my name!"

McKendree looked back in surprise and said, "William Hibbard is not your name?"

"No!"

"Then what is?"

"My name is Billy Hibbard!"

"Billy—Billy—" said McKendree in disgust. "That's the name of a small boy!"

"I know," answered Hibbard. "I was a small boy when my parents gave it to me!"

METHODISTS AND BLUE SPIDERS

Freeborn Garrettson was one of the pioneer founders of American Methodism. Bishop Asbury considered him one of his spiritual sons. Garrettson faced his share of persecution, having been beaten and even jailed for preaching. But when he led his young preachers up the Hudson River Valley, he met a new kind of resistance, especially by the Reformed Dutch clergy. They were fearful that their people would abandon the old church, and of course they were right. But the Dutch clergy weren't going to give up easily. They played upon the ignorance and superstition of their people, and spread tales about the dire consequences of hearing the Methodist preachers. One story had a sinister impact. The Dutch pastors cautioned their people to beware, for these Methodist preachers gained their converts by throwing blue spiders on the people while they were listening to the sermons!

History proves, however, that the threat didn't work, for Garrettson was able to plant Methodism from New York City to the Canadian border. Obviously the blue spiders had no taste for prospective Methodists.

THE 1796 RULES FOR METHODIST EDUCATION

Although the term *Methodist Seminaries* in 1796 included all institutions founded for the training of chiefly male Methodist youth, the General Conference's strict "29 Rules" for education are hard to square with the more permissive stance of education today. Just a sampling of the rules of 1796 will provoke a gasp even in the most rigid of today's Methodists, particularly the youth.

The students shall rise at five o'clock in the morning, summer and winter, at the sounding of a bell.

All the students shall assemble together at six o'clock for public prayer, except in cases of sickness; and on any omission shall be responsible to the master. (The rest of the day spent in study except for meals)

From evening prayer till bedtime, they shall be allowed recreation.

Their recreations shall be gardening, walking, riding, and bathing without doors; and the carpenter's, joiner's, cabinet-maker's, or turner's business, within doors.

A convenient bath shall be made for bathing.

A master shall be always present at the time of bathing. Only one shall bathe at a time; and no one shall remain in the water above a minute.

The students shall be indulged with nothing which the world calls play. Let this rule be observed with the strictest nicety; for those who play when they are young, will play when they are old.

The bishops shall examine, by themselves or their delegates, into the progress of all students in learning every half year, or oftener if possible.

Idleness, or any other fault, may be punished with confinement, according to the discretion of the master.

A convenient room shall be set apart as a place of confinement.

As demanding as these rules were, it is encouraging to note the broad philosophy of education at Cokesbury College, which was the first college founded by the Methodist Episcopal Church. The purpose of education there was to produce "rational scriptural Christians." In 1789, after visiting the school, Coke and Asbury reported their findings to "the Brethren." In part they wrote:

We had the pleasure at our last visitation, to observe several of the Youths displaying strength of memory, and propriety of pronunciation in their public speeches delivered in their Mother tongue; others discovering a considerable knowledge of the Latin and Greek classics, and others a mathematical genius. The industry and efforts of three of the youths in gardening, gave us no small satisfaction. Each of them chose his little spot in the rude state of Nature, fenced it, cleaned it, formed it into little beds and walks, and raised therein a variety of pleasing plants and vegetables. Above all, several of them have been, and now are, under gracious Impressions, and some truly converted to God. Four are boarded, and they and three more educated, gratis.

Your faithful Pastors,

Thomas Coke,
Francis Asbury

Those Shouting Methodists

The Wesleyan movement was energized by hymn singing. Nowhere was this more evident than in camp meeting. A camp meeting hymnal published at Richmond, Virginia, in 1807 offers examples of the basic theology and pride those Methodists shared.

> They pray, they sing, they preach the best.
> And do the Devil most molest,
> If Satan had his vicious way,
> He'd kill and damn them all today.
> They are despised by Satan's train,
> Because they shout and preach so plain,
> I'm bound to march in endless bliss,
> And die a shouting Methodist.

Another hymn carries the same sense of assurance with a touch of political conviction:

> The World, the Devil, and Tom Paine,
> Have try'd their force, but all in vain,
> They can't prevail, the reason is,
> The Lord defends the Methodist.

We can't imagine singing God's praises with such verses today, but we can appreciate the pride, identity, and loyalty aroused among the Methodists who "shouted" those hymns in 1807.

Methodist Lotteries and the Man in the Scarlet Coat

When British Captain Thomas Webb (1724–1796) first burst in upon the New York City Methodists worshiping in the rigging loft, they must have suffered a moment of panic. He must have seemed a frightening apparition dressed in full military uniform—scarlet coat, sword, and the eye patch that covered his wound from the French and Indian War in 1759.

The Methodists, however, had nothing to fear from Captain Webb, for they soon learned he was a spiritual son of John Wesley. Actually they quickly learned that his enthusiasm and energy would greatly further the Methodist movement.

Later when Webb was well established as a preacher in Philadelphia, he helped engineer the Methodist's purchase of the Dutch church which is known today as St. George's United Methodist Church. Actually he may have provided much of the purchase price from his own pocket. He was not adverse to emptying the pockets of others. The method he used was well established among Methodists of the day. It was lotteries. A letter Webb wrote December 27, 1771, to Daniel Montgomery, a Trustee of Old St. George's, tells the story.

> Brother Pilmoor wrote to me sometime ago that he would be glad to see me to consult about the lottery. If I could be of any service, I should be glad, if it is possible. I might dispose of a few tickets to some of my friends in the city. But this will be of little consequence unless the most of them are sold. I have a shorter and better way, viz: I am willing to be one of ten who shall take one or two and I think this number of persons (?) may be found to favour such a proposal. But if it should come to a point, I will go as far as three hundred in order that the lottery may be filled. You may propose this to Brother Boardman, and take his opinion. I think it would be better to push our friends than to drop the lottery.

It is an interesting footnote that at the General Conference of 1812 a Mr. Sales moved that lotteries be discontinued. The Conference voted to lay the question over to the next session in 1816. The Minutes of 1816, however, make no reference to lotteries. Apparently lotteries continued in use for some years as a tool of Christian Stewardship. What a contrast to "Methodist Morality" today when raffling a cake could be a slippery step toward hell!

——◆——

PASTORAL CARE—OLD STYLE

Philip William Otterbein (1726–1813) was a colleague of Asbury and founder of the Evangelical Church. One day in January of 1813 he received word that his cousin's wife and daughter had been burned to death in a fire in a theater in Richmond, Virginia, on December 26, 1812. Otterbein's letter of condolence reflects the attitude of the time. He no doubt thought he was being pastoral in his counsel, but imagine how contemporary pastoral caregivers would recoil from such thoughts.

Dear Cousin:

I lament the untimely death of your beloved wife and daughter. It is shocking to think of it. A hundred immortal souls have been hurried, and that unexpectedly, in less than an hour's time, into an awful eternity! Did that happen by chance? The wicked and unbelieving may imagine it. The Christian, who believes in a world-governing God, and in the divinity of the Bible, sees the hand of the Almighty, without whose will not one hair could fall from our head, even on such a calamitous night. Do the inhabitants of Richmond see this? I wish they may, but I fear not many will. The committee made a resolve to abstain from all worldly pleasure—dancing for example—for four months. Only four months! And what afterward? May they then play and dance again? It seems so. But this appears from another resolve: the committee hopes that their calamity will be a warning that no theater should be permitted to be opened until every facility has been provided for the escape of the audience. Oh shame! How God-offending and God-mocking is this resolve. If they had made a resolve against the building of another play-house they would have done honor to themselves, to God, and to religion.

What do you say, my dear cousin? You have lost a beloved wife and dear child. Do you see and feel the hand that lies so heavy on you? I know you do. But do you see and feel that terrible evil, the sin, that brought this calamity upon you? Awake! my dear cousin, awake. The Lord has blessed you with the temporal things of this world. But what are these but vanity? I know you would give your houses and all your silver if you could call back your wife and child. It is impossible. Thank God that you are alive yet. Adore the hand that has afflicted you. Pray for grace. Oh, don't neglect that! Cry aloud! The Lord is merciful Pray for grace to repent and believe.

W. Otterbein

No First-Class Inns

It is difficult for us to imagine the rough conditions many circuit riders faced on the frontier. They rode for miles on narrow trails. Facing natural as well as human dangers, in all kinds of weather, they often had no idea where their night's lodging would be. Usually at nightfall some family in the wilderness would take them in, and under less than pleasant conditions.

Just such an unhappy visit was described by a Rev. Bascom, "Tried to study, but too much confusion, tried to pray in the family, but felt too dull, tried to eat breakfast, but the victuals were too dirty for any decent man to eat. The old man is a an idiot, the old woman a scold, one son a drunkard, the other a sauce-box, and the daughter a mother without a husband."

Another story describes the food often offered the preacher. Rancid pork and johnny-cake were frequently the fare. One itinerant's appetite fled when he saw the soap kettle, boiling next to the dinner kettle over the fire, foam over into the stew.

No Match for Hungry Preachers

An army travels on its stomach and so did those early American soldiers for Christ, the Methodist preachers. Stories abound about their ravenous appetites especially for chicken and most any other food that didn't move.

A story about Jesse Lee and his cohorts underscores the point.

Lee, who weighed 259 pounds, told of the embarrassing moment when he and some of his preachers stopped at a farm at harvest time. Typical of the time, neighbors would gather to help with harvesting the crops. On this occasion a considerable group were assisting in the fields cutting the wheat. A long day would bring them to the table hungry for their meal. But the hungry Methodist preachers arrived first. They were seated at the table first and as Lee said, "we did full justice to the dinner prepared for the harvesters."

When the men from the fields finally got to the table, there was precious little left. The blessing offered by one of the harvesters said it all, "Oh Lord, look down on us poor sinners, for the Methodist preachers have come and et up our dinners. Amen."

CATCHING-UP ON THE LATE NEWS

One of the early circuit riders, J. V. Watson, was amazed at the ignorance of some of the people he met on his travels. Many people could not read or even write their name. Certainly they were out of touch with current affairs. But Watson had trouble believing the ignorance of one woman where he stopped. He asked her if she knew about Jesus dying for all of us. With some emotion she exclaimed, "Is he dead?—Well we had hearn out here of the death of Franklin, and Washin'ton, and all the great Indian fighters, but never knowed afore that Jesus was dead!"

BLACK HARRY HOSIER—THE AFRICAN WONDER (C. 1750–C. 1806)

Harry Hosier, familiarly called Black Harry, was an illiterate Methodist preacher of marvelous power and talent. Raised in slavery, freed, and converted to Methodism, Hosier became known as the African Wonder. Wherever he preached he was acclaimed by many as the greatest natural preacher they had ever heard. For several years he traveled and preached with Asbury and Garrettson

41

as well as numerous others of the prominent Methodist leaders.

As an African American, Hosier faced racial prejudice. One instance occurred in Hackettstown, New Jersey in 1803. Hosier was traveling the Trenton circuit with John Walker. A woman in the house where they were meeting said "she would not hear the black." Harry, hearing her remark, retired to a corner of the garden, and prayed with great fervor until the time for the meeting. During Walker's sermon Harry sat on a chair in front of him. When the sermon ended, Harry arose and, in the most humble manner, spoke of sin as a disease. All there were affected. Referring to himself, Hosier said that the Lord had sent a remedy by the hands of a physician, but alas, he was black. Some might reject the only means of cure because the hands by which it was sent to them were black. People were deeply moved especially the woman of the house, for she was converted by his message. In this case, prejudice was overcome by the power of Christ's love conveyed by the African Wonder.

PRACTICAL EVANGELISM

All preachers who believe God's Word is not rightly preached without careful exposition of the proper lesson from the Lectionary need to hear this story about Benjamin Abbott from the history of Methodism in Long Island, New York, in 1790.

Benjamin Abbott, who was prominent for his power if not for his polish or scholarship, raised the devil when he preached. After he finished his sermon, the members of his congregation were surprised that the windows weren't shattered and the shingles torn from the roof. Once Sunday he reached the climax in one of his tremendous sermons in the midst of a terrific thunder storm and cried out, "May God thunder on the outside while I thunder inside."

On one occasion Abbott took as his text Luke 19:21, "I feared thee because thou art an austere man. Thou collect what you did not deposit, and reap what you did not sow." But Abbott, with his usual power and conviction, read and believed he was right, "Thou art an oyster man." When reminded that he should have said, "austere man" and not talked so much about raking oysters, Abbott, undaunted, replied, "Never mind, Brother, we raked in seven sinners, didn't we?"

Score one for practical evangelism!

WORN-OUT PREACHERS

The Minutes of the 1796 General Conference shows the first use of the description, "Worn-out Preachers" to designate those who had to retire either because of age or infirmity. More often than not illness struck these preachers down. The itinerant ministry simply wore them out. In those days the churches took up a collection for the preachers and their wives to help with their support. When you learn the preacher's schedule, no wonder they were worn out. In a history of Methodism in Georgia and Florida for the years 1785–1865 there is careful summary of the circuit rider's life. It helps us understand why there were "worn out preachers."

> The daily and weekly schedule of the circuit rider was a strenuous one. The hour for rising was generally four o'clock, winter and summer. From that time until six the preacher read and prayed. After prayers with the family, and breakfast, he mounted his faithful horse and was off to his appointments. He preached about twelve o'clock, and invariably held class with his flock, whom he had not seen in twenty-eight days and would not see again for twenty-eight days more. He went home with some good brother, and frequently preached again at night. This he did every day in the week except Monday. If he had a wife, he tried to get to see her then; but generally he was single, and spent the day with his colleague. There was a conscientious exactness in filling appointments, and to do that he braved all weathers and dared all dangers. The rides were long, the exposure great, the labor exhausting, for he was generally a boisterous man. All this required men of iron, and but few preachers were able to endure it long; and health giving way, one by one they sank into their graves or retired from the work broken down in body.

Preachers on Trial

Although the nineteenth century saw many changes in the Methodist Episcopal Church, a vigorous moral and social code still applied to the preachers, their families, and church members even as in the century before. Though the moral code was well intended, this strictness led in later years to a kind of moralism which equated faith with keeping the rules. But in the early part of the nineteenth century the moral and social rules were rigidly applied.

The New York Conference trial records in 1813 indicate what was deemed important respecting the character and behavior of the proposed preacher, and his family. For instance, Mordecai Smith, a Long Island preacher, was recommended for a Circuit, but objection was raised in Conference concerning his lack of authority in his family. His wife and daughters wore gold jewelry. Brother Smith was a useful preacher. Therefore it was decided to elect him deacon on the condition that he exert authority in his marriage and family. He must correct the evils charged, especially respecting his younger children.

Another case was not so easily resolved. The Conference voted to reconsider the case of Brother Edmonds. One charge involved his having married contrary to his wife's parents consent. The second charge to which he confessed was that of light and trifling conduct. Edmonds also refused to pray in families and neglected to meet classes. To these charges he also confessed his guilt. He was also apparently an avid hunter and was charged with going hunting instead of "attending his appointments." He confessed to this charge, but offered the lame excuse that he didn't know of his appointments at the time. Then the Conference really got serious and charged that Edmond's wife dressed herself with rings, etc. What the *etc.* covered is not stated. To Edmond's everlasting credit he declared to the conference that "he liked to see her in such array."

The upshot of this encounter, according to the minutes, was that Edmonds was "To remain on trial."

Part Two

American Methodism
Growing as the Nation Grew
1816–1920

Introduction

The stories and anecdotes in this section begin with 1816, the year of Bishop Asbury's death. Although he was the principle founder of American Methodism, and the undeniable force in the spread of Methodism, his death did end the last significant leadership spawned by Wesleyan Methodism. Asbury's authoritative leadership style, though emulated by others, had made its mark. But now the episcopacy was in the hands of American Methodists. They were much better qualified to lead in a changing church and society.

Nineteenth-century Methodism was slowly changing its emphasis, form of worship, and the manner of living from that of the previous generation. This was due to a variety of factors. The world in which Methodism existed was different. Railroads, factories, western migration, and social problems such as slavery began to dominate the landscape. Methodism needed to adjust its message and habits to the new demands of a new society. Education was being emphasized. Slavery led to the division of the church, north and south, and later the division of the nation. In addition, gold was discovered in California, and the forty-niners forced change on the country. But Methodism was growing. More and more the Methodist Church was becoming the Protestant people's church. By mid-century its leadership had the ear of Presidents (Lincoln, Grant, McKinley). The domestic and foreign mission of the church significantly carried not only Methodism, but also Americanism, to our

47

own western frontiers and to other continents.

The stories and anecdotes continue to 1920. Although this year is a rather arbitrary choice, it may be argued that the Methodist Church in the opening decades of the twentieth century still had a powerful and respected voice on the American scene. Therefore all the more is it useful to examine what the people were like across these years 1816–1920. What were the bishops like? The pew-sitting people and their preachers. What was the power of this strange phenomenon called camp meeting? The struggle for women's rights in church and society? What about the church showing its muscle in prohibition and strike negotiations?

These stories are the heartbeat of who we Methodists were in those critical years of growth and change in church, nation, and world. Some of them might even be, as Chesterton said, "secret passwords" to be remembered as we make our way into the twenty-first century.

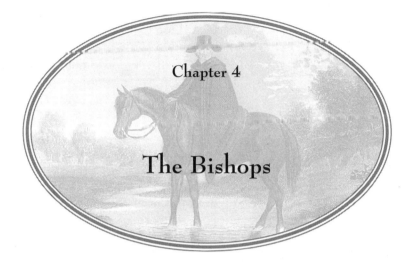

Chapter 4

The Bishops

"I Can't Beat You Because I Am a Bishop"

Henry Kumler Sr. (1775–1854), one of the pioneer bishops of the United Brethren Church, had numerous credits to his name and ministry. The United Brethren Church, which eventually merged with the Methodist Church in this century, elected its bishops at each General Conference. It was not a lifetime appointment. Henry Kumler Sr. broke that pattern by being elected bishop at four successive General Conferences beginning in 1829. His members were scattered through Pennsylvania, Virginia, and Ohio. In his first eight years as bishop, Kumler crossed the Alleghenies on horseback eighteen times. He traveled more than any other United Brethren bishop with the possible exception of Bishop Newcomer, his colleague.

During one of those eighteen trips across the mountains, Kumler, who was a rugged person, fell in with a pleasant stranger. They rode all day together. As evening came the bishop's companion drew a pistol, pointed it at him and demanded his money. Kumler grabbed the gun, taking the robber by surprise. Making as if to beat the man over the head, the robber pleaded that he was only joking and the gun was empty. Kumler was not amused. He gave the man a lecture and threatened to give him a thrashing. Only one thing saved the man. Kumler said, "I can't beat you because I am a bishop."

Kumler and his son, Henry Jr., held a unique record in the United Brethren Church, and possibly in the entire church. From 1841 to 1845 the Kumlers, father and son, were bishops at the same time.

A Humble Bishop but Not Much of a Preacher

The typical Methodist congregation in the nineteenth century, even as today, had varied expectations of the preacher and his sermons. In most cases moving eloquence filled the congregation's desires. But not all preachers were eloquent. He did, however, have a keen sense of humor as the following story illustrates:

> An eminent lawyer approached Bishop Roberts when they were both traveling on a Mississippi steamer. The lawyer asked him if he were acquainted with that able man, Bishop Soule, and that eloquent preacher, Dr. Emory. Upon Roberts replying that he knew them both well, the lawyer continued, "There was another, a old man, who preached not long since in our place; I think they called him Bishop Roberts; they say he is a most excellent man, but no great preacher—do you know him?"
>
> "Yes," said the old gentleman, "I have been acquainted with him for a good many years; I believe the old man is honest and tries to do the best he can, but you are right—he's not much of a preacher."

Roberts's saddlebags, his chair, and pocket watch are in the care of the United Methodist Archives. Dating from 1824, they are a reminder of this man's service to the church in Indiana and Methodism in general.

WILLIAM "CALIFORNIA" TAYLOR—
MISSIONARY BISHOP TO THE WORLD

John Wesley declared that "The world is my parish," but it was William Taylor (1821–1902), more than any other, who made the world the missionary parish of the Methodist Episcopal Church. His ministry represented the major missionary thrust of the Methodist Episcopal Church in the nineteenth century. At one time or another during his fifty-seven years of ministry, Taylor evangelized in Canada, Australia, Tasmania, New Zealand, Aukland, England, Ireland, Scotland, West Indies, Ceylon, India, Palestine, South America, and Africa. He gave his address as "the globe." But it all started in California.

Born 1821 in Virginia and converted at camp meeting, Taylor was a member of the Baltimore Conference. One of his first assignments was to California at the time of the gold rush in 1849. Arriving in San Francisco this giant of a man spent seven years in what was then a godless, lawless, and unrestrained city—a city of mushroom growth. Not only in his church, the first to be erected in San Francisco, but in parlors, brothels, jails, and gambling dens, among miners, sailors, merchants, and social outcasts, Taylor pointed the way to salvation. His street preaching drew thousands. Methodism in California was stamped with his energy and personality.

Taylor rolled logs all morning with the men, and preached to them in the afternoon. A logger in Red Holes said of Taylor, "If he's as good in the use of the Bible as he is with a handspike he'll do." Obviously he was an excellent preacher and became known as "California" Taylor or by many as "Father Taylor," not only in California, but all over the world.

THE SUNDAY SCHOOL BISHOP

John Heyl Vincent (1832–1920) began his ministry in Nutley, New Jersey, in 1853. The church, which he served there until 1857, bears his name—the Vincent United Methodist Church.

Early in his ministry Vincent became a pioneer in Christian education. He developed a unique hands-on Sunday School training program in biblical history called Palestine Classes. This interest in the Sunday School prompted him in 1861 to organize the first Sunday School Teachers Institute in America. As editor of Sunday School publications he introduced a system for printing lessons as separate pages.

Together with Lewis Miller, Vincent's crowning achievement was the founding in 1874 of the famed Chautauqua movement in New York State. Chautauqua continues today as a premier program in ecumenical religious, social, and artistic education.

Vincent was elected bishop in 1888. But his major contribution remains as a pioneer in Christian education. His efforts represented a singular shift from a rigid, revivalistic focus in the Sunday School curriculum toward a more humane, and psychologically sound approach particularly in respect to the Christian education of children.

Bishop Vincent deserves to be remembered as the Sunday School Bishop.

Pork Barrels, Preachers, and Appointments

Today the manner in which preachers are appointed to churches is often cynically viewed as a political process. In contrast many are inclined to believe that in the last century the guidance of the Holy Spirit was the chief force in appointing the preachers. This view, however, is not altogether accurate, especially when the practice of one bishop is noted. This bishop described, for his new presiding elders, his method in making appointments. He used the image of packing pork after slaughtering a hog.

The bishop pointed out that a farmer, after butchering the hog, carefully puts the inferior pieces of pork at the very bottom of the barrel. He then continues packing with grades of increasing quality until he reaches the top where he places the best parts of the hog. The farmer did this because he didn't like to eat the pig snouts until last.

The bishop then made the application of packing pork to the making of pastoral appointments. "Brothers," he said, "you begin by making two nominations for your District of two brethren about whom there can be no question. In this way we will continue through all the Districts until all such clear cases are exhausted, and then we will fix the places about whom we know there will be trouble. In other words, like the farmer, we will save the snouts till last."

WHEN ALL ELSE FAILS

One of our deeply pious nineteenth-century Methodist preachers, who later became a prominent bishop, was Philip Newman (1826–1899). His position was enhanced by having served as pastor of the Metropolitan Methodist Episcopal Church in Washington, D.C., chaplain of the U.S. Senate, and as pastor and friend to President Ulysses Simpson Grant.

Indicative of the position of influence Methodists enjoyed at that time in our country, Newman records in his unpublished journal an account of a special government mission he accompanied to Greenland as a part of the Polaris expedition to the Arctic. This was no doubt as a result of Newman's connection with the President. But in the same journal Newman, for all his influence and Methodist piety, revealed his priorities, "January 1871, Was vaccinated today. To cure my cold, took three pills, bathed my feet, packed my throat, drank lemonade, took snuff, and (finally) prayed."

Better late than never!

THE MACHINERY OF METHODISM

Bishop Matthew Simpson (1811–1884), friend of Lincoln and one of the most influential preachers of his time, had clear views about the nature of Methodism. In 1878, when preaching at Saint Paul's Methodist Episcopal Church in Newark, New Jersey, he spelled out what he saw to be the particular genius of Methodism.

He said, "As I understand Methodism, it is simply an organized method of carrying on revivals; it grew out of a revival, its whole machinery is the offspring of revival effort, and the system has become what it is because it was found to be what was needed, and what was most successful in promoting revival among the people."

Simpson's statement notwithstanding, the Methodist Episcopal Church, nonetheless, at that time was becoming more formal and structured in concerns for worship. This is well documented in respect to church architecture. By mid-century the church was offering plans for the building of formal and ornate sanctuaries. There was also a movement to establish orders of worship for Sunday Services. All of this was happening alongside a robust interest and growth in camp meeting. Revivalism and more established church forms and architecture were growing side by side, and Bishop Simpson was in the midst of the growth. It's puzzling, therefore, to read his further observation, "Methodism as a system has never carefully studied forms or ceremonies; its effort has been to get the world brought nearer to Christ, to find how to reach the heart of the masses."

A LEADER FOR THE TWENTIETH CENTURY

Bishop Francis John McConnell (August 18, 1871–August 18, 1953) was a true leader for Methodism in the early twentieth century. He was president of DePauw University from 1909 to 1912, when he was elected bishop. Quickly he became known as a social activist. From the beginning he was a leader of the Federation for Social Action from its founding in 1912. He became president of the Religious Education Association in 1916, and in 1929 was president of the Federal Council of the Churches of Christ in America. In 1919 McConnell gained national attention as chairman of the Interchurch World Movement Committee to investigate and report on the disruptive Pittsburgh steel strike. As a result he aided in eliminating the twelve-hour day in the steel mills.

Clearly in this Methodist bishop a new kind of church leadership had emerged which began to change the way in which the church

Famous Lincoln letter praising the Methodists.

looked at its role in defending human rights. McConnell's commitment to a more socially sensitive understanding of Christian responsibility set the stage for Methodism's more far-reaching view of the Church's political and social involvement in dealing with human rights in the twentieth century. Not only McConnell's example, but also his leadership have provided the high road the United Methodist Church travels in facing human need around the world.

Chapter 5

The Circuit Riders

THE PREACHER'S REVENGE

In the early years of the nineteenth century a typical pastoral appointment lasted two years. One would think in that short time one might hardly have time to find the post office, leave alone get to know the congregation.

This was not the case, however, in Morristown, New Jersey, in the early 1800s. The membership record kept by one pastor recorded his personal opinion of certain members of the church. He did this as a parting legacy to his successor with a view of being helpful.

After certain parishioners names were the unflattering evaluations as follows, "Expelled," "No good," "Good for nothing," "Lost or strayed." Then with deathly finality, he reported one brother who had "Gone to Hell."

It must be noted in fairness, however, that notes of appreciation were also left, "Good," "First-rate," "Can't be beat," and "Excellent." There is, however, no record of how the congregation rated the character and behavior of the preacher.

—————

The Circuit Riders

WHEN A FIRST SERMON COULD HAVE BEEN THE LAST

Many of the early preachers began their ministry with great enthusiasm, but with little training in sermonizing. One preacher, remembering his first preaching experience, probably never forgot the interruption that came at the high point of his sermon.

Recalling his first sermon he wrote, "I went through the preliminaries and took my text and began operation. It was a text which I have since found out that I did not understand, but it afforded me a basis for extended remarks. I used it a little like a cowboy uses a stob to which he fastens his lariat when he wants his pony to graze. It gives him latitude. So I fastened on to that text and grazed about it from all points of the compass. What I lacked in my knowledge of it I more than made up in the length of time I worked at it."

To the preacher's horror, just as he was reaching a heated and eloquent climax, Aunt Rachel Stone, a local eccentric, who "looked like the tallest woman I had ever seen," rose from her seat, deliberately strode up to the pulpit, shook her head and said, "Now, lookie here, my young man, ef you're a goin' to give it to us in that thar style I'll be switched ef I ain't got 'nuff of you jest right now." (Byrne, 217)

THOSE LONG-SUFFERING LAITY

It wasn't only the preachers who suffered with laypeople in the early days. The laypeople also had their problems, especially with novice preachers. In the early middle eighteenth century, beginning preachers were appointed to what were sometimes called calf pastures. Here the preacher and his wife were supposedly nurtured and raised up in the ways of ministry. But there were other preachers who weren't fledglings but had never learned how to get along with the people of their congregations. They had a way of creating trouble in their churches. One church in New Jersey had a preacher who became so annoyed with the congregation that he told the Official Board, "Of course, this church is only a second-rate appointment anyhow!" One quick-witted brother, who had had about enough, spoke up for the long-suffering congregation, "We are inclined to agree with you, considering the kind of preachers they send us."

Score one for the lay folk!

But sometimes the laypeople's only defense was to have fun with the very serious preachers. Henry Boehm, Asbury's traveling companion, told about the famous Jesse Lee. Lee came to a village one day and preached from the text Acts 17:6: "These that have turned the world upside down have come here also." Lee declared that through sin the world had been turned wrong side up, and it was the design of the gospel and the business of the ministry to restore the world to its original position. The next morning, after the sermon of the night before, nearly everything in town looked ridiculous. The wagons, the boats, the signs, and gates—anything that could be moved had been turned upside down. Boehm said, "The authors of the mischief enjoyed the fun, and laid it to the preacher, who they said had come to turn the town over so that it might be right side up."

KIDS AREN'T LIKE THEY USED TO BE

Nathan Bangs (1778–1862) was one of the founders of Methodism in Detroit while serving as a missionary in Western Canada. Later he gained prominence as an historian, preacher, and educator. But his prominence made no impact on some of the more youthful members in Detroit. Actually a story about Bangs's experience preaching in Detroit makes us thankful that the "kids aren't like they used to be."

During Nathan Bangs's sermon on the second trip he made to Detroit, a terrible storm with much thunder and lightning passed over the town. But Bangs kept on preaching with consistent steadiness. Afterwards he learned that he had been in great danger particularly when he took up the candle to read the closing hymn. Two young men had put gunpowder in the candles, expecting they would explode during the sermon. Nothing happened during the

Circuit rider.
(Source unknown)

service but the tricksters sat literally trembling in fear all through the storm because they thought God was about to strike them dead for what they had done. (Macmillan)

THOSE UNBELIEVABLE WESTERN PIONEER PREACHERS

Those Western pioneer Methodist preachers of the mid–nineteenth century were unbelievable. Hardship was their middle name, although they never used the word.

A news clipping describes the founding of Methodism in Wisconsin in 1837. In the fall of this year at the Illinois Conference, Frink received a "plum" appointment, the Sheboygan Mission. No small parish. It extended from the territory north of Milwaukee as far as Fond du Lac. He took hardship as a matter of course with no Pastor-Parish Committee to complain to, or 911 to dial.

Note his account: "I started for Sheboygan and at the close of the first day I found myself at Saukville. There I spent the night in an old shanty, putting my horse in one corner and barricading the door to keep out the wolves. There I endeavored to rest." The next day he traveled on to Sheboygan through wild and desolate country. There were no roads, no bridges, and he just swam his horse across rivers. Finally, he reached the Sheboygan appointment. The congregation appropriated $100 for his support.

The founding of Methodism in New Mexico wasn't much better. Brother Harwood was the founding preacher, and Father John Dyer his presiding elder. Dyer rode one hundred miles from Santa Fe to give Harwood his orders. After borrowing a horse and finding a saddle, Harwood eagerly asked about his field of labor. Dyer's reply grips the imagination: "Get your pony shod. Then start out northward via Fort Union, Cimarron, and Red River until you meet a Methodist coming this way. . . . thence westward and eastward until you meet other Methodist preachers coming this way. All this will be your work." Harwood, in a masterpiece of understatement, observed, "I saw at once that I had a big field."

Father John Dyer, known as the Peter Cartwright of the Rockies, founded Methodism in Colorado. In his autobiography is this choice story. "From Fair Play I went to Buckskin Joe, and with Brother Antis, held meetings for about two weeks, in the face of every kind of opposition—at least two Balls a week, a dancing-school, a one horse theater, two men shot. And yet, not withstanding all these things, we had a good meeting. The church was much revived, and several backsliders were reclaimed."

If you go to Fair Play today, you can visit Father Dyer's Chapel now open as a museum. It is an inspiration to all Methodists.

THEY HANGED THE PREACHER

We all know about the woman giving the apple to Adam, but what about a role reversal? The incident happened March 9, 1859, in New Jersey. Only this time the man giving the apple to the woman was a Methodist preacher.

Rev. Jacob S. Hardin, the first Pastor of the Anderson Methodist Episcopal Church, married a young woman from the congregation. Things apparently didn't turn out as well as he might have hoped and Hardin sought a way out of the marriage. Possibly after studying Genesis, he got the notion that an apple might do the trick. He tempted his bride with a poisoned apple and killed her.

Trying to escape conviction, Hardin left Anderson on March 14. After a frantic flight, he was finally captured in Virginia and

Reverend Gilbert Traveli—Modern day circuit rider, Arizona, early–twentieth century.

brought back to New Jersey. He was tried and hanged in Belvidere, New Jersey, the county seat of Warren County, on June 28, 1860. Hardin was twenty-three years old.

A FIGHTING PREACHER WHO PRAYED AFTER HE FIRED

Not all the preachers in the Civil War were chaplains. Some were in the front lines using their skills as sharpshooters. One of the unique and rather amusing examples of preacher/soldiers comes from Henry Howe's recollection of an Indiana regiment.

Howe remembers, "It was at Carrick's Ford in West Virginia, July 13, 1861. There was a Methodist preacher who was said to be one of the very best shots in the regiment. During the battle, he was particularly conspicuous for the zeal with which he kept up a constant fire. The Fourteenth Ohio regiment, in the thick of the fight, fired an average of eleven rounds to every man, but this parson managed to get in a great deal more than the average. He fired carefully, with perfect coolness, and always after a steady aim, and the boys declare that every time, as he took down his gun, after firing he added, 'And may the Lord have mercy on your soul.'"

What can be said but, "Pass the ammunition and then praise the Lord!"

An Unusual Argument for the Itinerancy: Fewer Sermons Are Needed

Itinerant preachers secretly knew that fewer sermons were required if they didn't have to preach to the same people year after year. The more a preacher moved, the fewer sermons he needed. Rehearse and rehash!

Here is the argument from the point of view of a hard working Methodist preacher and scholar, Jonathan T. Crane, the father of the author, Stephen Crane. Writing for the Methodist Quarterly Review in 1866, Crane made his point in an interesting fashion. He wrote:

> The itinerancy permits the minister to give his time and mental force to the preparation of a comparatively small number of sermons, and is therefore favorable to thorough preparation for the pulpit.

> If the preacher addresses the same people from year to year, how great the labor of keeping up the supply of new material. If he remains many years, how much strong argument, beautiful illustration, and fervent appeal, become useless after a single utterance. The itinerancy, by rendering it possible to use the same preparations more than once, gives time for thorough study. To enable a man to do his best in the construction of a sermon, he must have time to study his subject carefully, lay his plans deliberately, and work until he feels it is done. The itinerancy gives time to do this, and therefore has an advantage over the other system. It is a positive excellence of our system that it permits the minister to spend much labor on a comparatively small number of discourses.

However, Crane was not naïve. He recognized the power of human frailty, and the sin of laziness implicit in any system. Taking exception to his own words, he wrote:

> We know that, under any plan of ministerial labor, the hireling who careth not for the sheep will do his work with a slack hand. In the settled ministry, as it is called, he will put new texts at the head of old manuscripts, or preach as his own the sermons of better men. In the itinerancy he will repeat the same sermons, without addition or improvement. In each place, as the street musician grinds over before each house all the tunes that his organ can play.

Crane was at least a realist. He recognized that remaining in one church for years could lead to sermon rehash. But the itinerancy presented the same problem. One may conclude that Crane's aim was to challenge preachers to better sermon preparation. Such preparation, however, must not result in using a manuscript or even notes in the pulpit, for this practice was considered lacking in sincerity and orthodoxy.

THEY STOLE THE WRONG HORSE

An amusing story from Texan Methodist history involves a typical conflict with the Native Americans over horse stealing. One of the circuit-riding preachers followed such a regular route that his horse needed no direction. Knowing every ranch, the horse turned in every lane, and stopped at every ranch without prompting. One day a band of Indians rode through the settlement looking for horses. The preacher's horse was evidently a fine catch, and was quickly stolen. When the ranchers gathered, however, with a posse to pursue the horse thieves, the brave who had stolen the preacher's horse was in big trouble. His attempts at speedy flight were continually interrupted by this horse that stopped at every ranch and farm. The brave finally dismounted and ran for his life. (Egger, 92)

Reverend Frank Washington, black circuit rider, St. Helena Island, South Carolina.

HORSE STORIES

The Methodist saddlebag preachers, like cowboys, were wholly committed to their horses. It was no wonder because the nineteenth-century preacher, either by saddle horse or carriage, had no other way to reach the people. At Conference, after appointments were made, there would often be a great time of horse trading among the preachers. Those who were assigned to distant circuits would trade horses with those who were going to towns or villages where stronger horses would not be needed. The horse was appreciated.

James Erwin, for instance, highly praised his horse, Charley Black. Erwin, with a Paul Bunyan-like description, said that his horse was prepared for any emergency. He could "swim a river, soar over a mountain, skim the slough-holes, shoot over a floating log road, or out-distance a bear, or a pack of hungry wolves on a fair road."

Erwin further reported, "if we (the preachers) had but twenty-five cents we would spend it cheerfully for oats, and keep fast [a] day ourselves." To prove the point, an unnamed early bishop went so far as to pension his superannuated itinerant steed. (Byrne, 190)

ASSES AND HORSES

Lawyers and doctors enjoyed using the Methodist preachers as a butt for their practical jokes. Sometimes their habit of making fun of Methodist preachers backfired. In fact, when it came to lawyers and doctors, Methodist preachers could give as well as they got. A good example is a story about the Reverend John Ray, a circuit rider.

Ray usually rode a fine horse. On one occasion he was riding through town under the mischievous eyes of a group of young doctors and lawyers. Thinking to trap Ray, one of them called out, "Well, Father Ray, how is it that you are so much better off than your Master? He had to ride on an ass, but you are mounted on a very fine horse; you must be proud. Why don't you ride as did your Master?"

"For the simple reason," said Ray, "that there are no asses now to be obtained. They turn them all into lawyers and doctors."

NO CHARGE FOR WEDDINGS, BUT . . .

Some early preachers were clever bargainers. Their skill was often most apparent when they performed weddings. One preacher, when asked how much he charged for a wedding, made a shrewd response that put the groom in a corner. It always prompted a better-than-average fee.

"I don't make a charge," said the preacher, "but I allow the groom to measure his generosity by the estimate he puts on his bride. When I marry such a fine looking couple as you are, I always get five or ten dollars. But when I marry an indifferent looking couple, I don't expect more than two or three dollars."

Nearly always the groom went for the compliment, handing the preacher at least a five-dollar bill. That was a generous amount in those days.

False Teeth and Chicken Bones

Methodist preachers were notorious for their appetite for chicken. Whenever the Methodist preacher arrived, the lady of the house knew that she should seek out the fattest chicken to prepare for the preacher's dinner. Actually the chickens were reported to know a Methodist preacher on sight. Before he reached the farmhouse, the chickens would scatter into the brush knowing that their lives were on the line.

One story on this theme, although possibly apocryphal, tells of a preacher crossing a bridge over a creek. As he looked down at the water, his ill-fitting false teeth fell into the stream. He could see them, but couldn't reach them. He asked a lad, who was fishing in the stream, to retrieve the false teeth. The boy agreed saying, "It's deeper than you think, but I can get them. Where did you eat dinner?" The preacher replied, "At the Jones's."

The lad hurried away, returning with a chicken bone. He tied it to the end of his fishing line, and dropped it in the water. The false teeth snapped shut on the chicken bone. The teeth were neatly restored to the preacher's mouth. (Byrne, 256)

Some Strange Methodist Preachers

We all have our peculiarities. It's amusing, however, to reflect on this affliction when it emerges among preachers. Jacob Payton, reflecting on some of the strange preachers he had known, said:

Every Conference has its difficult preachers. They are hard to place. Often they are likeable and harmless and relieve the Conference dullness. But for the Cabinet these people are what is called problem preachers. Often the appointive powers attempt to explain away a preacher's weaknesses as mere foibles and divert attention by speaking of his dedicated wife. The final word in appeal to a Pulpit Committee is: "You know all of us have our peculiarities so do take him back another year."

There was such a peculiar preacher a number of years ago. Because his name was Kidney and because he moved every year he became known as "the floating Kidney."

In marked contrast, Payton remembered the consummate skills of another peculiar preacher, Sam Jones. Payton said:

After fifty years I can still see him delivering a lecture on total absti-nence. After scanning the gallery, the main floor and finally the platform as if trying to locate someone, Jones broke the inter-minable silence by saying, "I have just been looking you over, and I have concluded that the Devil is going to get most of you. But thank God, he'll not get much." The audience first gasped from sudden shock, then broke into gales of laughter. And after he had alternately convulsed his hearers with his humor, left them suffused in tears with his pathos, and set them aflame with indignation against the curse of intoxicants, they filed from the Hall saying that never before had they ever seen or heard the likes of Sam Jones.

"Here Am I, Lord, Send Me?"

Peter Cartwright was about as rough and tumble a preacher as they come. When he looked around him, he saw his fellow preachers enduring the same hardships and exhibiting the same perseverance. His description of them is not only an honest view of the way it was, but also a challenge for those who would follow now.

A Methodist preacher in those days, when he felt that God had called him to preach, instead of hunting up a college or Biblical Institute, hunted up a hardy pony of a horse, and some traveling apparatus, and with his library always at hand, namely Bible Hymn Book, and Discipline, he started, and with a text that never wore out nor grew stale, he cried, "Behold, the Lamb of God, that taketh away the sins of the world." In this way he went through storms of wind, hail, snow, and rain, climbed hills and mountains, traversed valleys, plunged through swamps, swam swollen streams, lay out all night, wet, weary, and hungry, held his horse by the bridle all night, or tied him to a limb, slept with his saddle blanket for a bed, his saddle or saddle-bags for his pillow, and his old big coat or blanket, if he had any, for a covering. Often he slept in dirty cabins, on earthen floors, before the fire; ate roasting ears for bread, drank butter-milk for coffee, or sage tea for imperial; took, with a hearty zest, deer or bear meat, or wild turkey, for breakfast, dinner, and supper, if he could get it. This was old-fashioned Methodist preacher fare and fortune. Under such circumstances, who among us would now say, "Here am I, Lord, send me?" (Strickland, 243)

The point Cartwright was making in this account is that times were changing, and the Methodist Church was changing. The church was becoming more established, appealing to a more cultured environment. To suit these changes Cartwright regretfully saw a new breed of preachers emerging.

Advice for the Art of Preaching

Amid the never ending flood of helps for preaching from "Snappy Sermon Starters" to "Aids for Preaching from the Lectionary," the advice given aspiring and beginning preachers in the early days is both interesting and amusing.

In his book on the folklore about Methodist itinerants, Donald Byrne mentions several choice and still useful pieces of advice. For example:

George Gary, about to ride to his first circuit, was told by a preacher, "Never pretend that you know much, or the people

THE FIRST METHODIST EPISCOPAL CHURCH IN AMERICA.

John Street old and new churches.

will soon find that you are sadly mistaken; neither tell them how little you know, for this they will find out soon enough."

Landon Taylor remembered advice given him when he began his ministerial career. An experienced pastor offered this practical counsel:

Be kind and pleasant always to the children, and not to abuse the dogs, lest you insult the owner. Be yourself, i.e. natural. Some young preachers seem to think they must assume a kind of preaching tone, which is unnatural. Be short. Never tell all you know in one sermon. Spare the Bible. Do not pound on it, for it is God's book; in this way you will show your reverence for his word, and your good sense. Quit when you are done, and don't annoy your congregation with useless repetitions.

Another experienced preacher advised, when asked how many sermons a preacher could make in a week, answered, "If he is an extraordinary man, he can make one; if he is mediocre, he can make two; but if he is an ass, he can make a dozen."

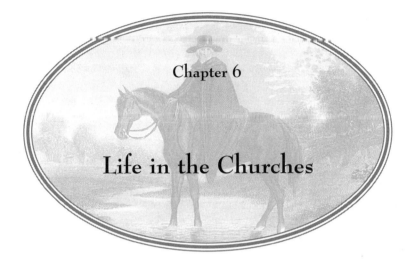

Chapter 6

Life in the Churches

CHANGES IN METHODIST PRACTICE IN THE NINETEENTH CENTURY

In the nineteenth century, and particularly during the post-Civil War period, Methodism went through tremendous changes. The worship services became more formalized, and changes were made in the structure and accouterments of the churches. Multiple keyboard organs, stained-glass windows, robed choirs, and cushioned pews became the pattern for many Methodist churches being built. Instead of small plain meeting houses, more churches were being built in the style of the Gothic revival and Romanesque architecture. Many of them were overbuilt in the sense that they provided seating for the great days of the church such as Christmas and Easter. At the same time, however, that such worship practices were being introduced in some parts of the nation, strong opposition to change remained. For instance, the use of the organ was strongly opposed. The famous Illinois preacher Peter Cartwright referred to the organ as the "squealing god." Another preacher in the Midwest arrived at his new appointment to find a pump organ in the church. He took it to the woodshed, like an errant child, and chopped it up.

It was only natural that the dress of both the laity and clergy should follow the ecclesiastical evolution. Except in unusual situations, gone was the simplicity of the early days. Earlier restrictions against finery and jewelry were relaxed and women wore hats of the latest style

71

rather than plain bonnets. Methodist men followed the general trend in men's clothing, wearing suits and ties, or what was called "Sunday-go-to-meeting clothes." Fancy dress was still frowned upon, for instance, suspenders were deplored. But with all the changes, the *Discipline* was slow in catching up. The old prohibitions persisted in the *Discipline* until 1852.

The clergy were now wearing black suits by which they were identified. In the pulpit or when conducting special services such as funerals or weddings, many preachers preferred Prince Albert coats, white vests and white bow ties. Gowns were not widely used and few ministers wore the clerical collar. As the century progressed, some of the preachers began to wear frock coats, striped trousers and winged collars in the pulpit and for special occasions.

The bishops had not as yet developed that sense of self importance that would cause them to dress differently from the regular preachers. But change was in the air.

THOSE VIOLENT, NOISY METHODISTS

Darris L. Egger gives an interesting account of the first Protestant preaching in what is now the Northwest Texas Conference. It was the 1820s, when Texas was still a part of Catholic New Spain, and the Methodist preacher was Rev. William Stevenson. Administering the first American colonies for the Catholic Mexican Government was Stevenson's friend from Missouri, Stephen F. Austin. Of course, it was dangerous to be anything other than Roman Catholic, but here was a Methodist preacher loose in the territory.

Austin's letter to his sister in 1824 states his view of those unwelcome Methodist preachers and their followers. Clearly Austin was trying to be tolerant of the Methodists, but was suggesting that they keep a low profile.

He obviously knew that this was not the usual Methodist practice, and that the typical Methodist behavior could lead to trouble for his administration among the Catholics.

I am of the opinion that no evils will arise from family or neighborhood worship . . . provided it is not done in a way to make a noise about public preaching, so as not to start excited Methodist preachers, for I do say that in some instances they are too fanatic, too violent and too noisy. . . . The subject of preaching must be managed with prudence, for I do assure you that it will not do to have the Methodist excitement raised in this country.

BEWARE OF HAVING A GOOD TIME

As the previous story illustrates those early-nineteenth-century Methodists were a straight-laced crowd. Step out of line, even to honor General Lafayette, and a person could be brought to church trial for frivolous behavior unbecoming a pious Methodist. Don't believe it? It happened at John Street Methodist Episcopal Church in New York City in 1824.

General Lafayette's triumphant tour to New York ended in a grand celebration at Castle Gardens. Sister Rachel, a member of the John Street congregation, because of her husband's political position was required to attend the party with her distinguished husband. The church worthies charged her with breaking Wesley's General Rule forbidding, "the taking of such diversions as cannot be used in the name of the Lord Jesus." She was brought to trial, but not expelled when she promised never to do it again.

A gentle cynic might observe that the real problem was that some of the saints of the church weren't themselves on the guest list for Castle Gardens. If they had been they might have taken a more lenient view of the whole affair.

BEWARE OF BAD BOOKS

Concern for the negative influences of literature and the media is nothing new. Methodists in 1854 were already being warned about the harm bad books could inflict upon one's mind and spirit.

A prominent publication, *Tracts of the Tract Society of the Methodist Episcopal Church*, reprinted a Tract entitled, "Beware of Bad Books," as a guide for all Methodists. The author defines what he means by bad books, namely:

> whatever books neither feed the mind nor purify the heart, but intoxicate the mind and corrupt the heart. Books of fiction, romance, infidelity, war, piracy, and murder are poison, more or less diluted, and are as much to be shunned as the drunkard's cup. They will bite like a serpent, and sting like an adder.

Without naming any specific books, the writer singled out for special condemnation "the foul and exciting romance." And why?

> The writer of modern romance chooses his scenes from the places of debauchery and crime, and familiarizes the reader with characters, sentiments, and events that should be known only to the police. Licentious scenes and obscene imagery are unblushingly introduced, and the imagination polluted by suggestions and descriptions revolting to the pure in heart. Mental delirium tremens is as sure a consequence of habitual intoxication from such reading as is that awful disease the certain end of the inebriate.

With a flourish come the closing words of the tract:

> Make this pledge before God: Henceforth I will beware of bad books, and never read what can intoxicate and deprave the mind and heart.

What a dent this plea would put on today's literary, film and TV fare! Where will Methodists go for entertainment?

—⟫◆⟪—

They Almost Ate the Old Woman

Many people in the early days of American Methodism were uneducated and often totally illiterate. Their ignorance often led to some amusing events.

Raybold, writing in 1849 about Methodism in West Jersey, recalled a tale from those early days which illustrates the illiteracy of many of the people. He tells of an old man, who upon the death of his wife, called his neighbors together for her funeral. The Methodist circuit rider never showed up, and the husband, in a quandary as to what to do, did the best he knew how.

Calling upon his meager remembrance of the Bible the old man said, "Well something must be done; the old woman must be buried." He began to say, "Our Father, who art in heaven, Now I lay me down to sleep," ending with "For what we are about to receive of thy creature comforts, O Lord, make us thankful." One lively person present exclaimed, "O dear! is he agoing to make us eat the old woman?" This was too much for the gravity of the crowd, and a shout of laughter followed.

The Old Wooden God

Peter Cartwright spent forty-five years serving in Illinois as a saddlebags preacher. He served in the state legislature and lost to Lincoln in a congressional race. No more feisty character rode the Methodist circuit, nor had more definite opinions about what was right in the church. He had little use for an educated ministry, and was particularly quick with his fists in dealing with those who attacked his preachers, or interfered with his camp meetings.

When Cartwright was attending a Conference in Boston in 1852, he unloaded on the Methodist worship practices he witnessed there, especially the use of the organ. He said to a preacher, "There's your old wooden god, the organ, bellowing up in the gallery, and a few dandified singers leading in the singing, and really do it all. The congregation won't sing, and when you pray, they sit instead of kneeling. We don't worship God in the west by proxy or substitution."

⤫ The Church Founded on the Gravel

We all know that Christ founded his church on the rock. But what about gravel?

From the days of the gold rush comes an amusing tale about the Downieville Methodist Episcopal Church in Sierra County, California. The church, organized about 1852, was built on unmined ground. The rich gold-bearing gravel under the church was twenty-five to thirty-five feet below ground level next to bedrock. At an unknown date some greedy person, hopefully not the preacher, tunnelled in from the river bank a hundred yards away and under-mined the church. Pillars were left to support the church while the gold-bearing gravel was removed. Of course every church needs its pillars, but in the pews, not underground.

But greed knows no bounds. The rascals came back, removing the pillars, to get the gravel at their base. Reinstalling the pillars, the tunnel was closed. With the installation of a new floor in the church in 1960, a cavity seven feet in diameter was found where the gold-bearing gravel had been removed. The Methodists never got the gold. Happily, the church was founded on Christ and is in good repair.

Musical Instruments and the Devil in Iowa

From the beginning, the Methodists cast a dim eye not only on fine clothes, jewelry, but also musical instruments. Such instruments smacked of the Devil's work. The only music in those early preaching services was a person leading the hymns without any musical accompaniment.

A good example of this controversy over the Devil's involvement with musical instruments, especially the organ, comes from a history of Iowa Methodism.

A pertinent variety of important Methodist scenes.

John Nye writes, "During the pastorate of O. C. Shelton at Agency in 1854, the first church building was erected. Not long afterward a controversy arose over the installation of a small reed organ. One group was very much opposed to the idea. They were sure that the devil would be let loose. Others prevailed, and the wooden music instrument was installed.

Michael See, who served in the Conference from 1845 to 1885, came to the church after an absence and was horrified to find a small reed organ in the sanctuary. He promptly rolled it out to the woodshed and chopped it up with an ax.

When people came to church that evening, the service was opened by the 'lining out' of hymns as usual. Nothing was said about the organ."

How to Hasten the Decline of Church Membership

At a time when church membership is declining, it is ludicrous to suggest ways of speeding the process. Imagine what would happen today if the rigid social discipline of the Methodist Episcopal Church of the past were imposed upon our members. There would be open rebellion, and an exodus of members. Probably many of our churches would be forced to close.

Note the evidence from the past. This was the Victorian period when the rules for moral and social conduct were rather firmly fixed. Methodism, like most denominations, did not hesitate to spell out the rules for the "good person." The *Discipline* for 1884 heralds the warnings concerning imprudent and un-Christian conduct:

> In cases of neglect of duties of any kind, imprudent conduct, indulging sinful temper or words, the buying, selling, or using intoxicating liquors as a beverage, signing petitions in favor of granting license for the sale of intoxicating liquors, becoming bondsmen for persons engaged in such traffic, renting property as a place in or on which to manufacture or sell intoxicating liquors, dancing, playing at games of chance, attending theaters, horse-races, circuses, dancing-parties, or patronizing dancing-schools, or taking such other amusements as are obviously of misleading or questionable moral tendency, or disobedience to the Order and Discipline of the Church—first, let private reproof be given by a Preacher or Leader, and if there be an acknowledgement of the fault, and proper humiliation, the person may be borne with. On a second offense, the Preacher or Leader may take one or two discreet Members of the Church. On a third offense, let him be brought to trial, and if found guilty, and there be no sign of real humiliation, he shall be expelled.

But it is important to recognize that the practices condemned in that time contributed to major social problems. This was the way the churches attempted to address them. Many of these practices, however, taken to excess are still with us, and perhaps, with greater impact, represent the major social and moral problems of our time.

METHODIST FAMILY LIFE—DIFFICULT TO BE A YOUTH

Strict, "Discipline-keeping" Methodists led an austere family life. It was hard enough for adults, but children and youth were carefully curtailed in their reading, their play, and leisure activities in general. Well into the twentieth century, especially on the Sabbath, children were forbidden riding a bicycle, or even looking at a Sunday newspaper. One was expected to sit quietly, read appropriate literature, or take a walk.

Two social activities, in particular, which were gaining popularity among the youth were denounced as the work of the Devil. One was skating, and the other was dancing. For instance, a church paper in 1885 printed a lead article: "Skating to Perdition," stating "The skating rink craze has become epidemic in this country, and is spreading in every direction in spite of righteous opposition." Declaring it to be worse than ordinary theater, one Methodist preacher told his congregation that "he knew of fourteen girls who had been ruined by these sinks of iniquity."

So no skating for Methodist teenagers!

And dancing? We all know how most youth love to dance. If you lived in the last century, and were a Methodist youth, forget dancing. The *Discipline* of the Methodist Episcopal Church forbids dancing, and the church media in 1900 denounced it as well.

The *Michigan Christian Advocate* had a scathing article entitled, "Is It Wrong To Attend the Dancing School?" In part the author wrote:

> The Bible clearly indicates that there is to be a dividing line between the world and the disciple of Christ. On which side is the dance?

> Are the low-cut dresses, bare arms and tightly clinging gowns befitting the modesty of one professing to be clothed in Christ's robe of righteousness? Can the giddy music, the overheated room, the early morning hour and the embrace of the opposite sex tend to purity of thought? Is the position assumed in the waltz tolerated in any other place? In a word, is it not all tending to temptation, if not actual

sin, and how can a Christian pray, "Lead us not into temptation," and then allow his children to go into the most captivating temptation ever invented?

Such racy denunciation sometimes has the reverse effect of making the forbidden attractive. But it is difficult to find any creative ways the church was providing to offer healthy counter activities to win the interest of youth in those years.

Answering an Atheist

Some say he was not an atheist, but rather an agnostic. There is a difference, but Robert Ingersoll did not always make that distinction clear. He was an outstanding political leader, and he might have been chosen for a presidential cabinet position in Washington had it not been for his unorthodox views on religion. Higher criticism of the Bible, for instance, was highly suspect, but Ingersoll made it one of his lecture topics. Because of his wit and his gifts as an orator, he was in constant demand as a lecturer, receiving sometimes thirty-five hundred dollars for an evening lecture—a truly fabulous fee in the nineteenth century.

On one occasion he proclaimed the death of the church, seeing in it neither a spark of life nor a will to grow. He was answered almost immediately by Charles McCabe (1836–1906), later Bishop McCabe but at that time in charge of the church extension work of the Methodist Episcopal Church. In answer to Ingersoll, McCabe sent him a now famous telegram "We're building two a day." This slogan became the watchword of the Methodist Episcopal Church, although there is no record that McCabe's slogan interfered in any way with the brilliant career of Ingersoll.

"O, Dry Bones, Hear the Word of the Lord"

Even if a preacher labored over his sermon, carefully shaping his argument, and illuminating it with pertinent illustrations, he might find himself preaching to "dry bones." But he still could hope that those bones might on some occasion come to life. A preacher at the Market Street Methodist Episcopal Church in Paterson, New Jersey, in 1881 kept a separate record of those in the congregation who needed special attention from his successors. There was a not-so-subtle inference that these church members did not deserve to be counted among the righteous until they shaped up.

The preacher carefully left his observations to guide future Pastors. His words:

To My Successor of Conference years 1881 forward—Brethren—

I had this Book made to order for the names of those only who are "Members in Full Connection"—I leave many names behind in the old Book—1st because they are unworthy to be continued among religious people; 2ndly because the old Book is still in use.

My scratching of such names simply means that they are not carried forward and not that they are dropped. . . . they stand there with the due record. . . . I had no right to scratch them in the sense of dropping them—but may the Lord help you to teach them as they deserve, if they ever do claim to be church worthies, until they repent and do right.

One wonders how effective the record proved in improving the spiritual health of those noted in the preacher's book of life.

Remedies and Cure-Alls

Methodists and other Christians didn't depend on faith alone for health and well-being. Evidence abounds in the advertisements in The *Christian Advocate*, Conference Journals, and other religious periodicals. The Methodists of the past were a ready market and target for any product promising health and beauty very much as we are today.

The *Christian Advocate* of January 21, 1886, offers a revealing example. A feature called "The Herald of Health" included the following: "How to Strengthen the Memory," "Nervous Exhaustion," "Controlling and Preventing Morbid Thoughts," "Ozone and Disease Consumption (Tuberculosis)," "Treatment for Feeble Children," "To Cure Cold Feet," "Cotton Seed Oil and Eggs as Foods," "Exercise for the Old," "Something about Cancer," and "Tired Eyes."

The same issue also offered an employment opportunity. The advertisement read, "Lady Agents Wanted: Sell the Girdle Health Corset. It conforms itself readily to large hips and busts." The Health Corset was recommended by physicians, but there are no before and after illustrations.

One product offered in this issue became a major American industry. Dr. Welch offered "Unfermented Wine—Pure For Sacramental and Medicinal Uses." Although a dentist, Welch's hobby was grape growing. His Methodist pastor in 1869 urged him to make a grape juice for Holy Communion replacing the customary wine. Welch gave up dentistry, bought two power presses and began selling grape juice to neighboring churches. He then developed a way to bottle the juice so that it could be shipped safely. Moving from Vineland, New Jersey, to Westfield, New York, the grape juice, jam and jelly business became the huge industry it is today.

Conference Journals also began to print commercial advertising. The New Jersey Annual Conference Journal for 1869 included a full page advertisement for Standard Home Remedies featuring Dr. Jayne's Family Medicines. The introduction states that these remedies are "admirably calculated to preserve the Health and remove disease. No family should be without them."

Some patent medicines offered were Jayne's Tonic Vermifuge, for Worms, Dyspepsia, Piles; Jayne's Alterative, Scrofula, for Goitre, Cancers, Diseases of the Skin and Bones; Jayne's Hair Tonic, for the Preservation, Beauty, Growth, and Restoration of the Hair.

Early advertisement for remedies and cure-alls.

The *Tennessee Methodist* for May 24, 1894 advertised a product that would sell as well today. It promised to help "THE TIRED BRAIN AND NERVES. Find the Sweetest, Safest and Best Relief by using Dr. King's ROYAL GERMETUER. It contains no Bromides, Cocaine, Chloral, or other Injurious drugs. Always safe for all ages and sexes. $1, or 6 for $5." A testimonial for this concoction adds this reassuring word: "Dr. L. D. Collins, Goldwaite, Tex. says of it: It is the finest Nerve Tranquilizer I have ever tried."

Such advertising for medical products became common. The *Christian Herald* for August 15, 1894 tempted the ill with a number of remedies for common health problems. Some typical remedies advertised with positive assurance were as follows: for "Piles [hemorrhoids] and all forms of Skin Diseases Positively Cured"; "Rupture Cured—With Our Improved Elastic Truss"; "Your Weight Reduced—15 lbs. a month by a new harmless, herbal remedy—safe, sure and speedy"; "Tape-Worm—Expelled alive in 60 minutes with head or no charge."

Another ad in this same issue of The *Christian Herald* offered treatment for cancer. This advertisement reads, "U.S. Census for one year, 1880, reports 35,007 DEATHS FROM CANCER. THE BERKSHIRE HILLS SANATORIUM, An institution for the thoroughly effective and perfectly scientific treatment of CANCER, TUMORS, and all malignant growths, WITHOUT THE USE OF THE KNIFE, WE HAVE NEVER FAILED TO EFFECT A PERMANENT CURE WHERE WE HAVE HAD A REASONABLE OPPORTUNITY FOR TREATMENT."

Those troubled with rheumatism should take note of the 1827 Minute Book of the Nutley, New Jersey, Vincent Memorial United Methodist Church. There among other important church matters is a remedy for rheumatism. Possibly the scribe was prompted by an agony of painful joints resulting from sitting at long church meetings. He felt, perhaps, obliged to offer other rheumatic church members some deserved relief. His remedy reads as follows: "Take a gallon jug. Fill it half full with spring water. Add one quart of good Holland Gin. Take a tumbler full as necessary." His remedy might not cure the rheumatism, but after a few tumblers full a sufferer might forget that he had the rheumatism—at least for a spell.

All of these remedies or cure-alls, although they may amuse us today, surely must arouse our compassion. Most of them were worthless, and the so-called medicines often depended on alcohol or some other tranquilizing drug as a base. Desperate and naive people turned anywhere for help, especially to remedies advertised in a Christian periodical. Obviously truth in advertising didn't exist.

A CURE FOR WITCHES

The subject of witches is a continuing theme in social and religious history. It is rare, however, that it appears in Methodism. Therefore, an unpublished journal of an early New England Methodist preacher is unique. He copied on the back cover of his journal a cure for witches which he claimed came from Cornwall, England. Apparently he kept it close at hand in case of desperate pastoral need. It is offered now just in case of emergency.

> Please to take a Bottle and put in 12 pins and 12 Truckles of White Thorns and 12 of Black Thorns. And one lock of your hair. Cut off the nails of your fingers and toes and put together. Bury it in the ground and do not tell anybody of it. When you lay it down, you must say these words: "You'll not rest Day or Night till you have righted me."

The cure closes with this final direction:

> Take a stone jar and fill it with urine and close it firm. Hang it up in the chimney with the mouth downward so as not to spill a drop of it.

Evidently this will do the trick though we've found no record of success or failure. Come to think about it there haven't been many witches around recently.

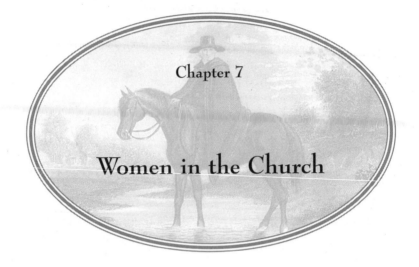

Chapter 7

Women in the Church

FEMALE FASHION FROM A MAN'S POINT OF VIEW

Today many of women's fashions are designed by men. In early Methodism the women's dress was criticized by the men, especially the clergy. The proof may be found in an article from the *New York Christian Advocate* for 1830 entitled, "Female Attire."

A nice attention to dress will cost much of what is more valuable than money, your precious time. It will too much occupy your thoughts, and that at the season when you would wish to have them otherwise engaged. And it certainly administers fuel to that latent fire of pride and vanity which is inseparable from our fallen nature, and is blown up into a blaze. I hope you will not be among the first of those who are eager to catch at and give sanction to every new mode; nor is it necessary, if the mode be decent and general, that you should be the last to adopt it. But something there should be in your exterior to indicate that though you do not affect a needless and scornful singularity, (which is often the source of censoriousness and envy), yet your heart is not set upon these little things. If a woman, when going to public worship, looks in the glass, and contemplates with self complacence the figure which it reflects to her view, I am afraid she is not in a frame of spirit most suitable for one who is about to cry for mercy as a miserable sinner.

Class in handwork, Fisk University, Nashville, Tennessee.

But I am not so much hurt by observing the materials, as by the manner of female dress—by what we call fashion and the eagerness with which changing fashion, however improper, is adopted by persons whose religious profession might lead us to hope they have no leisure to attend to such trifles. If some allowance is to be made for youth on this head, it is painful to see mothers, and sometimes possibly grandmothers, who seem by the gaudiness and levity of their attire, very unwilling to be sensible that they are growing older.

How interesting that this article makes no recognition that men had their own fashions and hair styles. We are led to believe that the men on their way to church never looked in the mirror to check their suit, tie, or hat.

What a revealing commentary on the view of women as persons. Of course, these views were solidly supported by the Discipline of the Church. The question was put: "Should we insist on the rules

87

concerning dress?" The answer: "By all means. This is no time to give encouragement to superfluity of apparel. Therefore receive none into the Church till they have left off superfluous ornaments." Obviously the rules were chiefly addressed to women, for the last rule states, "Give no tickets to any that wear high heads, enormous bonnets, ruffles, or rings."

WOMEN, DONKEYS, AND FOWLS

Women have not had an easy journey from the church kitchens to the church pulpits. Some denominations are still struggling with the issue. Surely Methodist women have their struggles. One of the early feminist stalwarts was a former slave, Jarena Lee. In 1849 when she heard objections to a female preaching, she had an answer that put the pious in their place. Lee said, "If an ass reproved Balaam, and a barn-door fowl reproved Peter, why shouldn't a women reprove sin? Maybe a speaking woman is like an ass, but I tell you one thing, the ass seen the angel when Balaam didn't."

A FORGOTTEN FEMINIST CHAMPION

Another Methodist woman who found her voice in the early 1820's was Sarah Low Norton. She never sought to become a preacher. That would hardly have happened that early. She was bright, an influential leader, and a friend to Bishops Asbury and Roberts.

Born in York County, Pennsylvania, in 1790 and raised in Kentucky, Norton in 1828 proclaimed a forward-looking message. She wrote, "I write just what I think. The world is not just to our sex and mind; its customs are tyrannical, and calculated to keep us almost dunces. The influence of women is I fear but the influence of material beauty. But this be it ever so great, is but dust in the balance compared to the charms of refined female intellect."

Women in the Church

METHODISTS AND WOMEN'S RIGHT TO VOTE

To our Methodist credit we should remember that the first women's rights convention was held in July 1848 at Seneca Falls, New York, in the Wesleyan Methodist Chapel. Sixty-eight women and thirty-two men signed a revolutionary declaration stating that "all men and women are created equal."

For over 150 years that Methodist chapel has housed everything from a place of worship to an opera house, a theater, a garage, and in a final incarnation, a laundromat. In 1993, however, the former chapel building was officially recognized as the birthplace of the women's rights movement. The washers and dryers were removed, the floor ripped up and the roof restored to its original height. A ribbon-cutting ceremony marked the addition of the chapel to the Women's Rights National Historical Park.

Just west of the chapel is Declaration Park. From a 138-foot fountain, water runs over a blue stone wall inscribed with the Declaration of Sentiments. This Declaration lists the rights denied nineteenth-century American women.

Methodists can take pride that these early beginnings of women's rights took place in a Methodist chapel. But we must remember our poor, though typical, social record respecting women in the earlier years of Methodism.

Our separation of men and women in worship services dated from the first *Discipline* in 1784. Patterned after Wesley's "Large Minutes" of the British Conference, Asbury and Coke agreed and asserted that such an arrangement was the universal practice of the primitive church. Using 1 Corinthians 14:40 they concluded: "A general mixture of the sexes in places of worship is obviously improper." The practice ceased in 1848.

Much has been accomplished since 1904 when women were finally received as delegates at General Conference. But we still have a long way to go in action and attitude.

—————>◦◇◦<—————

TOO BUSY FOR CHRIST AND THE CHURCH

In 1873 Annie Wittenmyer went after other women for having the wrong priorities. She had some cutting words for her peers in the Church.

> The time spent by the women of the church in dress and personal adornment—in useless and ornamental work—is almost incredible. I have known women in the Church to spend months of precious time over a piece of embroidery not much larger than a lady's pocket-handkerchief, and the while make excuse that they had no time for Christ's work. What a spectacle for heaven to look down upon!

A WOMAN SPEAKS OUT

Women were lobbying for official recognition by the Methodist Episcopal General Conference long before the decisive year of recognition in 1904. Laymen were received as official delegates to the General Conference in 1872. One of the sharpest statements respecting the rights of women in the church came in a statement addressed to the General Conference in 1880. Mary L. Griffith of Mauck Chunk, Pennsylvania, put forth the concerns of women. She wrote in part:

> The Church is supposed to be founded upon spiritual principles. Measured by a spiritual standard, women are the equals of men . . . Does His Church on earth fairly represent the kingdom when its constitution ignores woman, and its customs shut her out of its highest places of privilege[?]

> It rests with you, members of the General Conference, to remedy these evils, in great part, at least. . . . The masculine nouns and pronouns are used throughout the Discipline, in referring to these holding office—either lay or clerical—in the church. This is said to shut women out of all these offices. But this principle would also

Mother's class, Lebanon-Salem United Brethren Church, Pennsylvania, 1907.

shut them out of church membership altogether, for the General Rules declare the church to be "a company of men."

However, in order that the matter may be clearly understood, we ask you to formulate the principle, in legal, Disciplinary enactment, that the masculine nouns and pronouns, used in the Discipline of the M.E. Church, in referring to trustees, stewards, Sunday School Superintendents, class-leaders, exporters, and preachers—itinerant and local—shall not be construed as excluding women from these offices and, further, that the word "male" be expunged entirely from the Discipline.

We also ask that the General Conference shall recommend all our churches to devise or alter their constitutions and charters, so that the disabilities of women in all business meetings, may be removed.

Griffith's statement is unusual not only because of its forthright nature, but also because of its contemporary ring. Her insistence upon gender-inclusive language in the *Discipline* is far ahead of her time, and shows the distress and frustration some women felt in being left out of the official statements and organization of the Church.

"Go Forward or Renounce My Lord"
The Ordination of Women

In 1880 Anna Oliver read a paper entitled, "Test case on the ordination of women." Her statement reveals the social and cultural sacrifice facing Methodist women as they sought to answer God's call to ministry.

In part Anna Oliver wrote:

> I have made almost every conceivable sacrifice to do what I believe God's Will. Brought up in a conservative circle in New York City, that held it a disgrace for a woman to work. . . . I gave up home, friends, and support, . . . worked for several years to constant exhaustion, and suffered cold, hunger, and loneliness. The things hardest for me to bear were laid upon me. For two months my own mother did not speak to me. . . . And through all this time and today, I could turn off to positions of comparative ease and profit. However, I take no credit to myself for enduring these trials, because at every step it was plain to me, that I had no alternative but to go forward or renounce my Lord.

Oliver represented the inner conflict many women felt who struggled with a call to preach. They were scorned by the Church and often by family and friends. Today when nearly fifty percent of the students in many of our theological schools are women, we not only appreciate the pioneering role of Anna Oliver, but also her model of commitment and sacrifice.

Amanda Smith, evangelist, 1837–1915.

An Idiotic Fallacy

Frances Willard (1839–1898) was one of the most able persons in the Methodist Episcopal Church in her time. An educator, author, and reformer, Willard was especially known in the church and the nation as the founder of the Women's Christian Temperance Union. The temperance cause was critical, especially for the women, because of the destructive effect of alcohol usage in society, and especially in the family. But the WCTU had a broader philosophy than just opposition to alcohol. It was a movement for women's rights. The members sought to foster "a religion of the body." Willard encouraged men and women to give up alcohol and nicotine. She advanced a scientific gospel of proper diet, simplicity of

93

American Methodist Ladies' Association, 1866.

dress, abundant ventilation, and physical fitness. They insisted that healthy minds and healthy bodies were inextricably linked.

At the World's Columbian Exposition in Chicago, October 16–21, 1893, Willard, addressing the Women's Christian Temperance Union, did her best to lay to rest what she considered the "idiotic fallacy" respecting women. She said:

> Of all the fallacies ever concocted, none is more idiotic than the one indicated in the saying, "A woman's strength consists in her weakness." Let us insist first, last, and always that gentleness is never so attractive as when joined with strength, purity never so invincible as when leagued with intelligence, beauty never so charming as when it is seen to be the embellishment of reason and the concomitant of character. What we need to sound in the ears of girlhood is to be brave, and in the ears of boyhood to be gentle. There are not two sets of virtues; and there is but one greatness of

character; it is that of him (or her) who combines the noblest traits
of man and woman in nature, words, and deeds.

Just five years before her address to the Columbian Exposition,
Willard led a feminist charge at the Methodist Episcopal Church
1888 General Conference. She and seven other prominent Methodist
women gained election in their own Annual Conferences to be seated
as delegates at the General Conference. They were turned away.
Their presence prompted an address at the Conference entitled, "Are
Women Laymen?" This was an attempt to rationalize the exclusion
of women from the Conference on constitutional grounds. A footnote to this rejection of Willard and her cohorts turns on the person
of Angie Newman, one of the female delegates. It is interesting that
at that same Conference Angie's husband, Philip Newman, was
elected bishop. One can only imagine the dialogue that must have
occurred in their personal lives as the Conference progressed.

KITCHEN CANARIES AND THE LADIES AID

One distinguished Methodist Pastor in 1920 affectionately called
the women of his church, including his industrious wife, his
"Kitchen Canaries." After all they were the ones who cooked all
those church suppers. Their labor raised most of the money for the
church repairs, the parsonage furnishings, and mission support.

Of course, these women were proud members of the "Ladies
Aid." Where would the churches have been without this loyal band?
Incidently the pastor who coined the label "kitchen canaries" lived
to be one hundred years old. Obviously he gave up using the label
in recent decades else he would never have made the century mark.

Although the poetry leaves something to be desired, the
following piece recognizes the women's work from a humorous
perspective.

We've put a fine addition on the good old church at home,
It's just the latest kilter, with a gallery and a dome;
It seats a thousand people—finest church in all the town;

95

IF SADDLEBAGS COULD TALK

And when 'twas dedicated, we planked ten thousand down.
That is—we paid five thousand—every deacon did his best;
And the Ladies Aid Society, it promised all the rest.

We've got an organ in the church—very finest in the land,
It's got a hundred pipes or more, its melody is grand.
And when we sit in cushioned pews and hear that organ play,
It carries us to realms of bliss unnumbered miles away.
It cost a cool three thousand, but t'will stand the hardest test;
We'll pay a thousand on it—the Ladies Aid the rest.

They'll give a hundred socials, cantatas too, and teas;
They'll bake a thousand angel cakes and tons of cream they'll freeze;
They'll beg and scrape, and toil, and sweat for seven years or more,
And then they'll start all o'er again for a carpet on the floor.
No, it isn't just like digging out the money from your vest,
When the Ladies Aid gets busy, and says, "We'll pay the rest."

Of course we're proud of our big church, from pulpit up to spire;
It is the darling of our eyes, the crown of our desire;
But when I see the sisters work to raise the cash which lacks,
I sometimes feel the church is built on women's tired backs;
And sometimes I can't help thinking, when we reach the regions
   blest,
That men will get the toil and sweat—and the Ladies Aid the rest.

—Author Unknown

Chapter 8

Camp Meetings

INTO THE WOODS: CAMP MEETING STORIES

Camp meeting throughout the nineteenth century was the premier agency for evangelism. Bishop Asbury extolled the worth of camp meeting as "the great plow that tears all up by the roots. These meetings are our forts and fortifications." By the middle of the nineteenth century camp meeting became markedly institutionalized, reaching the point where manuals were published which outlined how the camp meeting grounds should be laid out and how far apart benches should be placed.

But camp meeting is a rich source of stories which reveal how Methodists worshiped and socialized. In the early part of the century these meetings provided opportunity for extreme emotionalism. An incident in 1810, for instance, chronicled in a treatise concerning an Albany, New York, camp meeting, illustrates camp meeting emotional fervor.

> After sermon, a prayer meeting was held in front of the stage, a bedlam of bedlam would be nothing compared to it—Some singing, some praying, some jumping, some clapping and wringing their hands: one falling here, another there, crying, "Glory to God, I am happy; the Lord has entered me"—then bursting forth in another place and singing—

Shout, shout, we are gaining ground; Glory, Hallelujah!

Satan's kingdom, 'twill come down; Glory, Hallelujah!

Another crying out, "We will pray old Satan's kingdom down— Blessed be God, brother, Satan can't stand here."

Some preachers went to any length to keep women in their place. Their place was definitely not in camp meeting leadership. Apparently some women in 1843 were getting a little too aggressive fancying themselves as preachers. Some men charged:

> Nature itself may be said to teach us that woman cannot quit her sphere of relative subordination with regard to man without dishonoring herself and losing her proper strength. The camp meeting encourages women to pray in public, and to address promiscuous (mixed) meetings, and by the spirit it infuses, makes them willing to unsex themselves in this way.

By the last quarter of the nineteenth century, however, more women were taking prominent leadership in camp meeting. Ossee Fitz-Gerald, the mother of Bishop James Fitz-Gerald, for instance, became a major leader of the Holiness movement, using the New Jersey Mt. Tabor camp meeting as her base of operation.

Lynch's Law and the Mormons

Camp meeting was not always a place of serenity and peace. The "Devil's camp" located on the outskirts of the meeting provided space for the scoffers to carry on. They would sell liquor, gamble, and generally tempt the faithful. Such ne'er-do-wells were a constant bother to the preachers. But on occasion the harmony of camp meeting would be disturbed by other religious groups who disagreed with the Methodists. One amusing experience of this nature may be found in the autobiography of Peter Cartwright, who was famous for rugged behavior. He had no problem with dissidents. Cartwright

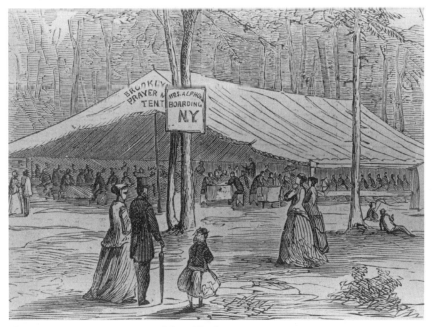

Camp meeting prayer tent, New York.

described one camp meeting that "was numerously attended, and had a good and gracious work of religion going on among the people." Then a group of Mormons tried to break up the meeting. They were no match for this "wild man" preacher.

> An old lady Mormon began to shout and speak in an unknown tongue. Just then my attention was drawn to the matter. I saw in one moment that the whole maneuver was intended to break up the good of our meeting. I took hold of the old lady's arm and ordered her to hush that gibberish; that I would have no more of it; that it was presumptuous, and blasphemous nonsense. She took me by the hand and said, "I have a message directly from God for you." I said, "I will have none of your messages. If God can speak through no better medium than an old, hypocritical, lying woman, I will hear nothing of it."

Camp meeting.

Cartwright brought the episode to an end with these words, "This is my camp meeting and I will maintain the good order of it. Don't show your face here again, nor one of the Mormons. If you do, you will get Lynch's Law." Tranquility returned, and Cartwright reported, "They all disappeared, and a great many were converted to God, and the church was revived and built up in her holy faith."

Peace, harmony, and love of Jesus apparently returned to the camp meeting services as soon as Cartwright threatened to hang the Mormons.

No Nose for Watermelon

As camp-meeting grounds became by mid-century a place for summer retreat and renewal, not all residents were simply in search of spiritual renewal. Social times and recreation became of central importance. Along with such socialization, some amusing contradictions occurred. At one campground in the 1870s the literature sternly announced that no liquor was allowed on the grounds. The notice warned that the camp meeting superintendent had such "strong olfactory senses that he could smell liquor a rifle shot away." But it was common knowledge that you could have a bottle of liquor delivered in a hollowed out watermelon. Obviously the superintendent didn't have a nose for watermelon!

With Fits and Jerks

When people come together for meetings intended to stimulate religious revival, unusual emotional and physical expressions often occurred. Camp meeting was famous for the exhibition of such behavior. Nowhere is this phenomenon better described than in Peter Cartwright's autobiography.

> Just in the midst of our controversies on the subject of the powerful exercises among the people under preaching, a new exercise broke out among us, called the jerks, which was overwhelming in its effects upon the bodies and minds of the people. No matter whether they were saints or sinners, they would be taken under a warm song or sermon, and seized with a convulsive jerking all over, which they could not by any possibility avoid, and the more they resisted the more they jerked. If they would not strive against it and pray in good earnest, the jerking would usually abate. I have seen more than five hundred persons jerking at one time in my large congregations. Most usually persons taken with the jerks, to obtain relief would rise up and dance. Some would run, but could not get away. Some would resist; on such the jerks were generally very severe.

From our vantage point today we may find it difficult to determine the psychological explanation of such extremes as Cartwright described. Were these expressions of near hysteria? Were they demonstrations of authentic religious experience? But whatever our evaluation, times have not changed, for the fits, the jerks, and even barking may be observed in contemporary revival and healing services.

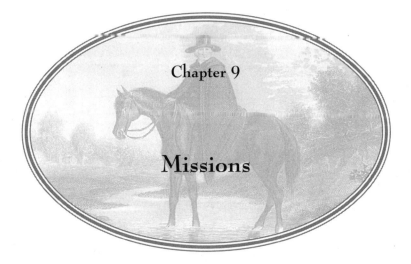

Chapter 9

Missions

THE BEGINNINGS OF METHODIST FOREIGN MISSIONS

Both home and foreign missionary work developed slowly in England and America. Bishop Thomas Coke (1747–1814) was probably the most missionary-minded of the English preachers. He carried the gospel into the Caribbean and died while on his way to establishing the Methodist work in India.

In America, home missions were started by a man named John Stewart. It is said he was converted while drunk. The conversion stuck, and he became a Methodist. Later he carried the gospel to the Indians in Ohio. In 1815, with rare tact and understanding, he came among the Indians while he was singing. Had they not liked his singing they might have scalped him for his bold intrusion. But they liked his music well enough to allow him to preach, and he began Methodist work among the Wyandot Indians. In 1819 the mission was adopted by the Ohio Conference, and on April 5 of the same year the Methodist Missionary Society was organized in New York.

The first foreign missionary of American Methodism was Melville Cox, who went to Liberia in 1833. He was sent out only after repeatedly urging the Methodists to proclaim the gospel in Africa. Cox's health was such that the Methodists hesitated to send him abroad,

Burning idols in Angola, early–twentieth century.

believing that his weak constitution would not stand the strain of the work. However, Cox's earnest spirit and his persistence won the day. He became the first missionary of American Methodism to serve in this way.

His friends, however, had been right in their estimate of Cox's health. He lived only four months after reaching Africa. His dying words became a rallying cry for all of Methodism: "Let a thousand fall before Africa be given up!"

BETHEL SHIP—METHODISM'S NAVY

Today many do not know that Methodism once had a Navy consisting of one condemned brig which never hoisted anchor.

This Methodist ark, called *Bethel Ship*, was commissioned *John Wesley*. It did not sail, but remained tied at Pier 11 in the North

River at the foot of Carlisle Street in New York City. Here in 1845 was established the "1st North River Bethel Ship Society of the Methodist Episcopal Church." The founding Pastor, Olaf Hedstrom, provided a church home and family to thousands of Scandinavian immigrants. Many of them were sailors. But the most illustrious convert was Jenny Lind, the "Swedish Nightingale," whose international fame as a singer was legendary.

The *Bethel Ship* ministry was unique, influencing countless ordinary Scandinavian immigrants. Many of them moved across the nation founding settlements, especially in the Midwest. Many returned to their native countries carrying their Methodist beliefs with them. Through their efforts, Methodism was founded in 1853 in Norway, in Sweden in 1854, and in Denmark in 1858. It is difficult to measure the impact of the evangelistic ministry begun on *Bethel Ship* except to note that by 1924, those efforts which had begun in 1845 had spawned four Annual Conferences including two missionary conferences, 217 churches, 128 preachers, and 20,000 members.

What an accomplishment for a one-ship navy!

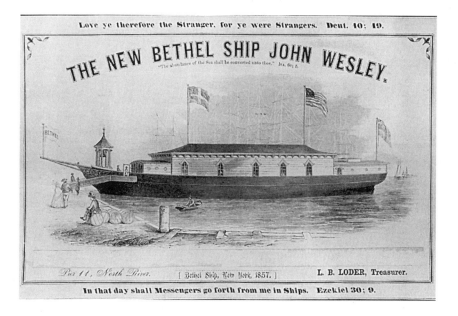

When Seeds Bear Fruit

Henry Gerhard Appenzeller (1858–1902) was a founder of Methodism in Korea. Entering Drew Theological Seminary in 1882, he became interested in mission work in Japan and Korea. After seminary Appenzeller fulfilled his dream, and founded the first Methodist Church in Seoul, Korea. He literally gave his life to Korea, founding churches and publishing agencies, and supporting Christian education. In 1902 he died in an accident while on his way to Mokpo.

The Appenzeller story has an inspiring turn. While at Drew, he served the New Jersey Greenvillage United Methodist Church in 1884. Recently, the Reverend Grace Chong, a native Korean and graduate of Drew, served that same church.

Appenzeller sowed the seeds of Methodism in Korea over one hundred years ago. Could he have ever dreamed that a female Korean Methodist pastor would serve the Green Village Church he served? Or could he have dreamed that Hae-Jong Kim, a member of the Northern New Jersey Conference and graduate of Drew, would become the first Korean to be elected a bishop in American Methodism?

Seeds have a way of bearing fruit, especially when they are sown and nurtured in Christian love.

Another Kind of Social Gospel

A circuit rider in the Evangelical Association, Matthias Hoehn (1826–1916), preaching among the Germans in Ohio and Illinois, records in his unpublished autobiography some strange social preaching he observed in his travels. It wasn't slavery or alcohol that drew the fire of the preachers he heard. It was the women's dress and the men's beards and side whiskers that drew criticism, becoming the point of sermons.

Here is Hoehn's description.

The sermons which these men preached, illiterate as they were, consisted largely of criticisms and condemnations about the style

106

in women's clothes and the whiskers worn by the men, . . . most uncouth and vulgar language was used in these denunciations. For instance, a woman's full blouse was called or compared to a "cow's udder"; the full sleeves, some kind of a bag; the tightly laced waists, a "sow-snout," and other parts of a woman's clothing were called "prostitutes vanities" and the devil's fripperies. For a man to wear a full beard or side whiskers, was enough to ostracize him (to) say nothing of his wearing a mustache. One man said, that if, for instance, the head of a man with whiskers would be found on the road one would not know whether it had belonged to a man or an animal. Of course, this sort of language was not general, but it did occur, and it seemed that the coarser the expressions, the more applause was forthcoming, for it provoked a great deal of laughter and amusement.

The Hand of God or the Hand of Theodore Roosevelt?

The United Methodist Church today often comes under criticism for meddling in politics, and for not paying attention to its true business—religion. During the Civil War, and then in the closing years of the nineteenth century, Methodist leadership appeared to welcome the partnership of government and church. This was particularly true when it afforded an avenue for foreign missions. Can you imagine Methodist leadership today interpreting war as the hand of God opening up a country for Protestant missions? It happened—and not that long ago.

The Spanish-American War in 1898 and our involvement in the Philippines was seen by the Methodist Episcopal Board of Missions as the work of God. A Board Secretary, Adna Leonard, (from 1888 to 1912, and then elected a bishop) so interpreted these events.

J. T. Copplestone gives an account of this almost unbelievable episode in our Methodist history.

He [Leonard] believed that through the operation of Dewey's squadron, the United States was thrust out into the Philippines by an overruling Providence, to break the power of Spanish despotism

New York City, World War I.

and to advance the missionary cause. In this Leonard saw the hand of God—not the hand of Theodore Roosevelt, Assistant Secretary of the Navy. Roosevelt had schemed, several months before the declaration of war (April 25), to get Dewey put in charge of the Asiatic Squadron. He cabled Dewey (behind the back of the more conservative Secretary of the Navy) to concentrate his squadron in Hong Kong . . . to see that the Spanish squadron does not leave the Asiatic coast, and then (begin) offensive operations in the Philippine Islands.

It happened just as Roosevelt planned. The Methodist Board of Missions responded with an editorial rejoicing in the new partnership between the armed state and the church. In part it read:

Assuming that Dewey has captured Manila and the flag of our country is today floating there, we are no longer compelled to go to a foreign country to seek raw heathen. When patriotism and evangelism can go hand in hand, the one strengthens the other. If it should result that the Philippine Islands are to remain under a protectorate of this country for years to come, it will be our immediate duty to establish a Mission there. And how glorious it will be to think that we have one Mission in the heathen world with the starry flag above it. (Barclay, 171, 172)

"THE METHODIST CHURCH IS NOTHING BUT A POLITICAL PROHIBITION PARTY!"

Some clergy of at least one other denomination in 1920 viewed the Methodist Episcopal Church as a political prohibition party.

Could this have been true? It is understandable. After all, the bishops of the Church at the General Conference of 1908 declared that, "The Methodist Episcopal Church is a Temperance Society." It is only a quick step from this view to a vigorous alliance between the Church and the Anti-Saloon League. Such an alliance mounted a political campaign which secured a constitutional amendment on January 16, 1920 making prohibition the law of the land.

No wonder some saw the Methodist Church as a political prohibition party!

Methodists have a long history respecting temperance or more precisely total abstinence. From 1850 forward, opposition to the use of beverage alcohol increased until it became, in the 1920s, the major social concern of the Church.

There were a few exceptions. For instance, in the early part of the nineteenth century there were two Methodist churches in New York City that boasted wine cellars in their basements. Particularly unique was a motion defeated at the General Conference of 1812 which, if it had passed, would have penalized a preacher for selling liquor. No one has explained these seeming inconsistencies.

The prohibition amendment, a major source of social and religious controversy, was repealed in 1932. The official attitude of the Methodist Church, however, remained in favor of total abstinence for Methodist clergy and laity alike. In recent years the Methodist

Mount Vernon Place, Baltimore, World War I.

emphasis has been on education and alcohol-related problems, recognizing that alcoholism is still a major national health problem.

It is improbable that many Methodists would vote today for national prohibition or even less probable raise their voices in singing a temperance hymn of earlier years called the "Water Drinker."

I am a drinker of water clear,
And never take spirit, or wine, or beer;
My eye sparkles bright, 'Tis not swollen or red,
And my step is steady, my path to tread;
My hands are not shaking, like those who oft sip,
And my nose does not look all red at the tip;
When morning returning bids sleeper awake,
My brain is quite cool, and my head does not ache.

A METHODIST MEMORIAL

In the museum area at the Commission on United Methodist Archives and History building at Drew University in Madison, New Jersey, is a little-known Methodist memorial. It is a rolltop desk. Two items displayed on this desk reveal its significance. The first is a photo of the desk's owner, Dr. Frank Mason North (1850–1935). Dr. North was the celebrated secretary of the New York City Church Extension and Missionary Society of the Methodist Episcopal Church, an organization which continued the work of those who carried the message of the gospel into each new frontier as the nation grew.

The second is a framed manuscript copy of a hymn North wrote at this desk in 1903. This hymn, "Where Cross the Crowded Ways of Life," captures North's passion for the city and the hurting peoples of the world. It remains a timeless expression of the social gospel and serves as a fitting coda for the history of American Methodism, which the stories and anecdotes in this volume have revealed. In the words of this hymn we find the Methodist sense of mission that the circuit riders carried to city, farm, and village in their saddlebags.

Where cross the crowded ways of life,
Where sound the cries of race and clan,
Above the noise of selfish strife,
We hear Thy voice, O Son of man!

In haunts of wretchedness and need,
On shadowed thresholds dark with fears,
From paths where hide the lures of greed,
We catch the vision of Thy tears.

From tender childhood's helplessness,
From woman's grief, man's burdened toil.
From famished souls, from sorrow's stress.
Thy heart has never known recoil.

O Master, from the mountain side,
Make haste to heal these hearts of pain;
Among these restless throngs abide,
O tread the city's streets again.

Bibliography

Barclay, Wade Crawford. *History of Methodist Missions,* Volume IV. New York: Board of Missions and Church Extension of the Methodist Church, 1949.

Byrne, Donald. *No Foot of Land: Folklore of Methodist Itinerants.* Metuchen, N. J.: The Scarecrow Press, 1975.

Egger, Darris L. *Prairie Parsons.* Abilene District of United Methodist Church, 1990–1992. Northwest Texas Conference, United Methodist Church.

Harmon, Nolan B., Ed. et al., *Encyclopedia of World Methodism,* United Methodist Publishing House, 1974.

Macmillan, Margaret B. *The Methodist Church in Michigan.* Michigan Area Historical Society, 1967–1976.

Nevin, John W. *The Anxious Bench.* German Reformed Church, 1844.

Nye, John A. *Between the Rivers: A History of Iowa United Methodism*. Publisher: Commission on Archives and History. Iowa Annual Conference of the United Methodist Church, 1986.

Raybold, G. A. *Reminiscences of Methodism in West Jersey*. Lane and Scott, 1849.

Strickland, W. P., Editor. *Autobiography of Peter Cartwright*. New York: Carleton and Lanahan, 1856.

Telford, John. *Wesley Anecdotes*. The Religious Tract Society, St. Pauls Churchyard. Pardon & Sons, Printers, Wine Office Court, Fleet Street, London, No Date.

Tyerman, Reverend L. *Life and Times of the Reverend John Wesley, M. A.* New York: Harper and Brothers, Franklin Square, 1872.

All illustrations are from the United Methodist Archives and History Collection and are used by permission.

About the Authors

Frederick E. Maser and Robert Drew Simpson are distinguished Methodist scholars and historians, having served over a period of seven decades as ministers, writers, teachers, and collectors.

Frederick E. Maser received an A.B. from Union College in Schenectady, New York, an M.A. from Princeton University, and a Th.M. from Princeton Theological Seminary. Maser served Methodist churches in Pennsylvania from 1933–1967. He was a district superintendent in the Eastern Pennsylvania area for several years and was pastor of Old St. George's United Methodist Church in Philadelphia, Pennsylvania. He also served as dean of students at Conwell School of Theology and as executive secretary of the World

Methodist Historical Society. A theologian and historian, Maser is the author of a book on John Wesley's sisters entitled *Seven Sisters in Search of Love* (The Foundery Press, 1990), *Little Known Appearances of Jesus* (Academy Books, 1996), and numerous articles and pamphlets. In 1977, his large Wesleyana collection, along with his collection of Anglican prayer books, was presented to Drew University. An amateur bookbinder, Maser donated his early-American bookbindings collection to Bryn Mawr College, and established the Mary Louise Jarden and Frederick E. Maser Book Fund for the preservation and expansion of the collection. Maser is now retired and divides his time between Doylestown, Pennsylvania, and Scottsdale, Arizona.

Robert Drew Simpson received an A.B. from Drew University and a B.D. from Drew Theological Seminary. He did graduate work at Union Theological Seminary, Columbia University, Cambridge, Oxford, and

Bristol Universities, and received a Ph.D. from Drew University in 1954. The grandnephew of Daniel Drew, Dr. Simpson has served as a trustee to the university since 1977. He is a member of the staff of the United Methodist Commission on Archives and History and teaches Practice of Ministry for Drew Theological School. A retired minister, Dr. Simpson served the Northern New Jersey Conference for forty-nine years. His published works include *Freeborn Garrettson, American Methodist Pioneer* (American Theological Association, 1954), *The Life and Journals of the Reverend Freeborn Garrettson* (Academy Books, 1984), and *The Civil War Letters of John Z. Drake* (1997). Dr. Simpson lives in Branchburg, New Jersey.